Covid Chronicles

ANTHONY FAUST

Lyla and Violet, thank you for ripping the links off our paper chain as I completed chapters. All my motivation comes from you. You can do anything you set as a goal. I am so proud of you two.

Thank you for your support, Jennifer. Thanks for letting me read chapters out loud to you, and for pretending to listen. Thanks for your honest feedback. I love you.

Table of Contents

Acknowledgements

This book was conceived in the MSP airport in April 2022.
These people helped me along the way:

Scott Dawson & Corinne Dawson
Jennifer Faust
Lyla Faust
Stan & Judy Faust
Violet Faust
Sharon Hagopian
John & Amanda Hobot
Mike & Katie Karnik
Josh Kociemba
Andy Loehrer
James & Krystal Luhrs
James McMahon
Jacque & Kate Marcotte
Derek & Holly Midas
Jeremy & Charlene Millincek
Jonathan Miller
Dustin & Jessica Miller
Bill Millinczek
Kyle Morehouse
Jason & Jessica Pavelka
Garrett & Greta Zimmerman

Special thank you to my sister, Jessica Pavelka, for helping me
proofread and edit this book.

Introduction

I am a husband and a father of 10- and 13-year-old girls. Like many, I was greatly affected by the COVID-19 pandemic. I was sent home from my job with my laptop on March 11, 2020, and have not been back into my company's office space since. Like everyone reading this book, it was challenging to adapt to the new world COVID-19 pandemic brought with it.

We did some amazing things during the pandemic response. I have fond memories of doing drive-by birthdays for my kid's friends. I remember the exact spot I was on my jog when I found a hand painted rock that read "We are in this together!" and it was so genuinely touching. I had regular Zoom happy hours with a close group of friends. I will never forget that unique experience.

I got to spend so much quality time with my wife, kids, and family.

For all the good, there was also a lot of negatives. I helped my youngest daughter do her daily math homework during distance learning. I saw how frustrated she got when she was trying to finish a session on a terribly designed application on her iPad.

I saw both girls deal with wearing masks while playing sports. Face masks do not belong on young kids when they are running up and down the basketball court. Or skating on the ice. Or in school.

And I watched our leaders politicize COVID-19. Making and changing policies that didn't seem founded in facts repeatedly. I watched small businesses permanently shut their doors. I watched the richest people in America accumulate insane amounts of wealth.

My intention with this book is to document some of the things we did, so we would remember it in the future. History repeats itself. The next time we encounter something like COVID-19, I hope some of the lessons we learned in this book help us make better decisions, and not repeat some the mistakes. It was a fun project to work on.

Enjoy.

Sports

Doubles Tennis Was Banned and Every Other Court Was Shut Down

One of the great outdoor sports is tennis. The very nature of tennis, with big courts and lots of space without direct person-to-person contact, tennis players can enjoy the many physical and mental benefits that tennis offers while maintaining six feet physical distance. For this reason, it was one of the few sports that didn't get completely shut down and was a good way of getting outdoor exercise while remaining safe from the spread of COVID-19.

Still, some facilities felt the need to put their own restrictions on the sports. Some of the strategies included but were not limited to: making users play every-other court to leave a buffer, prohibiting doubles matches, and requiring players to wear protective masks.

Here was the guidance from the United States Tennis Association:

• Wash your hands with soap and water (for 20 seconds or longer), or use a hand sanitizer if soap and water are not readily available, before going to court
• Avoid touching court gates, fences, benches, etc.
• Try to stay at least six feet apart from other players. Do not make physical contact with them (such as shaking hands or a high-five).
• After playing, leave the court as soon as reasonably possible.
• When playing doubles, coordinate with your partner to maintain physical distancing.
• No extra-curricular or social activity should take place. No congregation after playing. All players should leave the facility immediately after play.
• While there is no evidence that COVID-19 can be transmitted by touching tennis balls, sanitary precautions, such as handwashing, should still be taken.

The last one is kind of the kicker. There was no evidence that COVID-19 can be transmitted by surfaces, but these precautions were all recommended, nonetheless.

Golf Courses Added Foam Hole Fillers to the Cups

After COVID-19 hit in the Spring of 2020, opportunities to get out of the house were shrinking. Gyms were closing, swimming laps at the local YMCA was out of the question, even the early morning mall walker crowd was out of luck as these businesses were considered non-essential. For the middle age and beyond crowd, the number of ways to get some exercise was dwindling. There was one exception to this rule: golf.

Golf is one of the most popular sports in the United States. According to the National Golf Foundation, nearly 25 million people played golf on a golf course in the United States in 2020. That's around 8 percent of the total population of the U.S. which is a pretty large number all things considered.

Due to the demand of golfers, it was always going to be difficult to keep people off the course. Golf is also one of the most socially distancing sports you can play. Even in a foursome, golfers rarely need to be within 6 feet of each other. During the tee shots, every individual stands far apart from each other. The drives usually send each golfer down their own path of locating and eying up their mid-range shots. Most courses changed golf cart rentals to be one golfer per cart. This sped up the pace of play because you could zip right to your ball without having to locate a second ball for your cart mate. The second rule that was changed was no more raking the bunkers after putting a ball in the sand. It was deemed too high risk to have a golfer from one group smooth out their footsteps in the bunker and then have another golfer later come and use the same rake to clean up their mess as well. So, the bunkers remained ungroomed.

Ultimately, the group of golfers will convene on the putting green. This is where the silliest modification came into play. Some courses removed the flagsticks. Some of the courses required that no one remove the flagsticks because you didn't want two different golfers touching the same flag stick. Many of the courses added foam inserts to the holes, to make it easier to retrieve your ball without having to pull the pin. It robbed 25 million people golfers of the beautifully satisfying sound of the ball dropping to the bottom of the cup after nailing a 20-foot putt.

Basketball Rims Got Removed from Outdoor Courts

In spring of 2020, as soon as it became mildly warm and dry enough outside to leave the comfy stir-crazy confines of our house, my two daughters and I bravely headed outside for some exercise and fresh air. We grabbed a couple of outdoor basketballs and headed up the road to one of the elementary schools in our city with the largest outdoor basketball courts. It was a nice day, mid 50's if I recall, and we were excited to be getting out of the house together to get some exercise maybe play a little H-O-R-S-E, or Around the World.

When we showed up to the school, we parked and made our way around the back of the school where the playground and basketball courts were located. As we walked around the corner, we were greeted with police-style Do Not Cross yellow tape wrapping its way all over the playground. Up the ladders, down the slides, and around the merry-go-round. This was a bad omen.

As we walked to the court, dribbling, and chatting, we noticed the courts were completely empty. This was unusual as the courts usually had a half-dozen or more kids shooting on the two full courts with four baskets. This was great, we were going to have the courts all to ourselves! And then, we saw. The school district, in their infinite wisdom, decided that the best way to stop the spread of this disease was to...remove the basketball rims.

They had tasked someone in the maintenance team to go out to the playgrounds and unfasten the rim and net from the backboard, leaving four square as the only available activity on the playground. I think that if they had more time or thought it out more, they would have painted over the four square courts, too.

We just wanted to get outside, get some exercise, and return to what was a normal activity. Instead, we turned around and headed back to the car. We drove to the other two schools in the district and a couple other city owned parks. All had one thing in common: the basketball rims were no longer attached to the rims. Dejected, we returned home, and back to our hibernation cave.

Well done, school district and city leaders.

Skate Parks Were Closed and
Filled Up With Sand

COVID-19 arguably hit our nation's youth the hardest. They went through one of the most difficult school years possible. They went long periods of time without sports or extracurricular activities. Many families prevented their kids from getting together with their friends. A lot of popular youth hangout locations, such as parks, movie theaters, and malls were all shut down or severely restricted. Many youths were forced to sit at home and crush Netflix and *Call of Duty*, in an endless loop of monotony.

It was time to get the youth out of the house!

For those who enjoyed skateboarding, skateparks were an oasis in a dessert of conformity. In the 1950s, skateboarding was created created in Southern California, as an off-shoot of surfing, for something to do when the waves weren't crashing.

The popularity of the sport continued to skyrocket over the next several decades. In 2020, for the first time, skateboarding was an Olympic event (those Tokyo games were delayed until 2021, due to the pandemic).

With over 3 million youth skateboarders, the number of skateparks in America rose to over 3,500 in 2019, with over 77% of those using the parks being age 18 and under.

Skateparks are a place where the youth can go and hang out with their friends. They use it as a place to develop their athletic skills, build self-confidence, and strengthen social bonds. To them, skateparks mean everything. During the pandemic, many municipalities decided that the skater's haven needed to be shut down to slow the spread of the disease.

Rather than just post signs, many cities went to the extra measure to bring in sand by the tonnage and cover the whole skatepark with an unavoidable obstacle. Because, you know, we can't trust the kids to obey rules. For these youth, their identity was in a real way erased, and the sanctuary where they could be among their peers during a very frustrating, trying time was eliminated.

Youth Basketball Required Masks and Extra Policies for Spectators

In the winter of 2020, my oldest daughter was in 5th grade basketball. Covid restrictions had quite an impact on the basketball season. When we dropped the girls off for evening practice, parents were not allowed into the school. All the girls were required to wear face masks from the entrance to the gym, and there was a hall monitor to make sure they obeyed.

Once in the gym, all the girls and the two coaches were required to wear a mask during the entire practice. School district officials warned that they would be monitoring the practices and ensuring the rules were followed.

On weekends, the girls had tournaments. Here is the tableau of these tournaments: the team would meet in the parking lot. They would have their game time and wouldn't be allowed in the host school prior to their game time. When it was time to play, the girls would enter as a group, follow the arrows to their assigned court, and would be masked up the whole time. Only one parent was allowed to spectate. No grandparents, siblings, or any other people were allowed to watch, and those allowed in had to wear masks. The referees wore masks, with their whistles hidden underneath. As soon as the game was over, the girls were whisked away, out a deactivated emergency exit backdoor that dumped into the parking lot.

If your team happened to play on the same court in back-to-back games, here was the funniest detail. A janitor came over to the bleachers. He asked everyone sitting on the portable metal bleachers to stand up. Then he came along and wiped down the bleacher with Lysol, so each of the parents could sit right back down in their same seats. The janitor just gave a shrug as if to say, "I know this is maybe the stupidest thing in the world, but I'm just going along with it."

Across the country, there were plenty of instances of youths fainting, passing out, and collapsing while playing similar tournament. These girls were busting their butts up and down the court, fighting for loose balls, and gasping like crazy because they had something restricting their breathing the whole time. It's a wonder there weren't more issues.

Indoor Water Parks Added Extra Safety Measures

In the winter of 2020, there were still quite a lot of restrictions on businesses. Our family got invited to a 10-year old's birthday party, and a lot of the things you would normally do to celebrate that milestone were still closed. Bowling alleys, escape rooms, and video game arcades were all still shut down. Hotels never really closed, and as luck would have it, there was a great hotel in our area that has a huge indoor water park, with several tube water slides, splash pad for the toddlers and a lazy river and huge hot tub for the parents to enjoy. These hotel/waterparks are very popular in cold weather northern states because they let you escape the drudgery of bitter cold winters, even if it's just for just a quick weekend visit.

At this hotel, they hadn't quite figured out how they were going to operate during COVID-19. The waterpark portion of the property had been closed in the spring like everything else in the country. It took them about six months to figure out how to open the waterpark, and when they did, it brought a lot of pent-up families out of their house to do anything other than sit at home.

We checked into our room and immediately everyone in our party changed into swimming gear and headed down to the waterpark. Here is where it got a little silly. The hotel management opened one of their banquet rooms to serve as the entrance to the waterpark area. They used a second otherwise-out-of-the-way door as the exit. Each door was one-way only, so that the people entering would not have to cross paths with the people exiting. While you were walking to and from the entrance/exit, you were required to wear a face mask. The parents were casually sitting around tables trying to have a conversation, but indoor waterparks are notoriously the loudest places on the planet, and to try and have a conversation through a mask was quite a challenge.

When the kids came out of the water for a drink or snack, they had to immediately mask up. The lifeguards were tasked equally with watching the water for safety, and making sure the out-of-water children were wearing masks. But when the kids entered the water, they didn't have to wear masks! There is no bigger petri dish of activity than a waterpark, even with the chlorine and chemicals in the water.

An NBA Player Got Caught
Breaking the Rules in the
Bubble

The National Basketball Association (NBA) season was one professional sports league that got creative in playing through the pandemic. The 2019-2020 season was halted on March 11, 2020, and the league began to craft their plan. On June 4, the NBA's Board of Governors approved a plan to restart the season on July 30, which included a single site campus at Walt Disney Resort in Florida.

The 22 teams that were within playoff contention were brought to the campus, with players, coaches, and staff kept in a "bubble". They would play a short schedule of seeding games to determine the playoff teams, and then begin a playoff schedule to determine a champion in October.

There were strict health and safety protocols set in place. Everyone was tested daily for COVID-19. No fans were allowed to attend the games, and participants' families and friends were only allowed into the "bubble" after the playoffs' first round. They would stay and be held to the same precautions as the players and coaches.

The seeding games ended, and the playoff matchups were set. The Houston Rockets and Los Angeles Lakers advanced to the second round and matched up in the Western Conference Semifinals.

The day after game 2, reserve forward Danuel House Jr. got caught bringing an unauthorized guest--one of the female temperature checkers--up to his room for several hours. He was held out of games 3 and 4 while the NBA concluded their investigation and then was sent home. The Rockets would go on to lose to the eventual champion in five games. Shortly after, House got support from fellow NBA player Kevin Durant, while appearing on The Joe Budden Podcast. Durant said:

"If you've been in a bubble away from some action for
three months? I mean, you can't blame him, dog. I heard it
was no females at all outside of [COVID testers]. The
maids were all men, there was nothing but men around.
After a couple months, you down 3-1? Nah. 'I don't give a f
— no more man.'"

Professional Sports Played in Empty Arenas

The National Basketball Association (NBA) was the first league affected by the pandemic. The 2019-2020 season was suspended on March 11, and restarted more than 100 days later, on July 7, in the bubble in Orlando, with a limited few (mainly media and team executives) in attendance. As you watched the games on TV, these few spectators sat just out of frame on the near side of the court. You could tell some people were sitting there, but you couldn't quite see who, or how many. The cameras never shot that reverse angle. The gym had the feeling of a dark Division II college arena, with a super fancy video board and snazzy graphics alongside the court.

The good part was you felt like you were kind of in a practice session. The microphones could pick up more on-court chatter, and it felt intimate. The play was pretty good throughout the playoffs. As the rounds continued, rules relaxed, and some family members were able to join the bubble.

The Finals were not great. LeBron James and the Los Angeles Lakers beat his old team, the Miami Heat, 4-2. It felt anti-climactic, like the real accomplishment was completing the season successfully with few issues along the way, and that all the players were ready to go home.

The National Hockey League (NHL) also held their playoffs in a bubble, restarting on July 26 in two different locations: Toronto and Edmonton, Alberta. The league made the decision to host the games in Canada, as their coronavirus rates were much lower. They tried to recreate the arena experience, with simulated crowd noises provided by video game maker Electronic Arts and pre-recorded team specific chants, but those efforts didn't quite mask the feeling of an empty crowd. Playoff hockey is normally a crazy environment, and home crowd can really swing a playoff series. But not when there are zero spectators. The television production was very good, as they were able to shoot angles that are normally impossible with a crowd in the stands. The players could also be heard, with a 5-second TV delay.

The NHL wasn't very transparent with their players and a lot of the players spoke negatively of the league and their time in the bubble. After the Tampa Bay Lightning beat the Dallas Stars in six games, both teams seemed ready for the bubble to be over.

Paddleboarder Was Chased and Arrested Off the Coast of Malibu

During the first month of COVID-19, some of the states adopted all sorts of stay-at-home orders. California was one of the first states to come cracking down on what citizens were allowed to do. On March 19, 2020, Governor Gavin Newsom issued a stay-at-home order to protect the health and well-being of all Californians and to establish consistency across the state to slow the spread of COVID-19. At the time, people feared that the virus might enter the ocean water and be spread along the coast through the air.

On March 27, Los Angeles County closed all its beaches to reduce crowds as officials tried to slow the spread of the coronavirus. County Supervisor Janice Hahn said, "The crowds we saw at our beaches last weekend were unacceptable. To save lives, beaches in L.A. County will be temporarily closed. We cannot risk another sunny weekend with crowds at the beach spreading this virus."

On April 2, a man was arrested paddleboarding alone in the ocean off the coast of Malibu. He was doing stand-up paddleboard (SUP) surfing, and there was nobody else in the water, so he had the waves all to himself for over an hour. The county lifeguards (think *Baywatch*) were patrolling the area in a boat near the Malibu pier.

After refusing their orders to leave the water for 30 minutes, the lifeguards eventually flagged down Los Angeles County sheriff's deputies who responded by boat to help. This interaction was captured on video and it lives online. The situation is so surreal, it's hard to believe. The Sheriff's boat comes in hot, as if they are running down a drug smuggling cigar boat off the coast of Miami. In reality, they are aggressively chasing down and apprehending a single man on paddleboard, who isn't harming or bothering another single person on the entire planet.

The man made his way to the beach and was arrested and handcuffed on suspicion of disobeying a lifeguard and violating the Governor's stay-at-home order. It could be argued that going paddleboarding alone in the middle of the ocean could be considered the ultimate social distancing act, but the man faces a $1,000 fine, 6 months in jail, or both, if convicted of violating the state order.

Peloton Bike Sales Went Through the Roof

The COVID-19 pandemic has changed the way we live our lives in many ways. One of the most noticeable changes is how people are exercising. With gyms and fitness studios closed due to social distancing measures, more and more people turned to home workouts as an alternative. And one product that saw a massive surge in sales during this time is Peloton bikes.

Peloton was founded in 2012 by John Foley, a former executive at Barnes & Noble, and launched its first bike in 2014. The bike had a tablet attached to it which allowed users to access live classes taught by professional instructors streamed directly into your home. Users could also take pre-recorded classes with an instructor as well as compete against other riders in leaderboards. In 2018 they released their Tread treadmill, expanding their range of products even further.

Since its launch, Peloton's popularity had steadily grown over time even before the global pandemic struck, but 2020 saw an exponential increase in sales for them due to the closure of gyms around the world and health authorities advising against going outside for exercise when possible. In April 2020 alone, sales surged 300% compared to April 2019 as people sought out ways to stay active while being confined indoors for long periods of time.

This increase in demand has seen Peloton become one of the most valuable private companies in America with a valuation of more than $8 billion USD and its stock price soaring from $20 USD per share when it went public in September 2019 to nearly $171 USD per share by June 2021. This spike can be attributed largely to their latest product releases.

Peloton was one of the most successful businesses during this unique period where staying healthy was paramount to everyone's mind while still having fun exercising without leaving your own house. Peloton offered something unique that no other competitor could provide: interactive classes combining music, gaming elements and instruction delivered directly into your living room – perfect for anyone wanting to stay fit during lockdown.

NASCAR Made Their Drivers
Wear Mask

NASCAR drivers were forced to adapt to their new normal in the 2020 season, and that included wearing masks at the track. As the United States entered a pandemic-induced lock down in March, NASCAR was one of the first major sporting leagues to enact protocols for its athletes.

The mask requirement had been in place ever since NASCAR resumed racing in May of 2020 following a two-month break because of the COVID-19 pandemic. NASCAR drivers were required to wear masks when in close contact with other people and when not inside their vehicles.

The crew members also had to wear masks when they were in the garage or pits.

Many fans applauded NASCARS's ongoing effort to keep the event safe for all the employees and crew members that participate in race day. To other fans, it was a weird or even ridiculous site to make the drivers put on a mask in an open-air track without any fans in attendance.

As part of NASCAR's safety measures, individuals entering a track's infield tunnel to reach the garages were subjected to a screening process that involved checking their temperatures, credentials, and completing health questionnaires. However, two individuals affiliated with the sport recounted incidents where they were able to access the tunnel without being stopped or screened.

At first there was some confusion about where exactly these masks needed to be worn and how secure they needed to be. Some teams thought it was enough just to keep them around the neck or even tucked into shirts and jerseys, to NASCAR's chagrin.

NASCAR also had problems with some its drivers adhering to the rules and on several occasions, their drivers were seen maskless and gloveless chatting up the fans in the crowd.

In large part, the fans of NASCAR didn't really care. Categorically, NASCAR's fanbase was more of a 'Covid is just another flu' type of people, who didn't really take to the extra rules too kindly.

High School Hockey Players
Wore Face Masks
During Games

The 2020-2021 high school hockey season was one that no one could have dreamed of. With the outbreak of COVID-19, teams had to adjust their game plan to stay safe and healthy on the ice. One of the most immediate adaptations made by players and coaches alike was for all players to wear masks during practices and games.

At first, many players were less than thrilled about having to wear a mask while playing hockey - a sport that is typically fast paced and requires deep breaths to keep up with the action. Even so, everyone adapted quickly as it became clear that wearing a mask was necessary to protect themselves and their teammates from the virus.

As soon as they heard about the implementation of masks on the ice, they began preparing for what would be an entirely new experience for them all. Players discussed how best to make sure they were able to breathe correctly while wearing their masks; coaches developed plans for practice drills that worked with the extra layer; and administrators stocked up on extra masks just in case someone forgot theirs at home. It wasn't an easy transition, but everyone was determined to persevere through it for the sake of their own safety.

Not only did players have to adjust their physical game play when wearing masks, but they also had to adapt mentally as well. Hockey has always been a mental game—with split second decisions needing to be made on where and when you can move on the ice—but with a mask this became even more difficult. The fogging up of face masks due to condensation from breath caused by face coverings made it harder for some players to see. Coaches spent extra time during practices teaching players how best to control their breathing while skating around and playing defense so as not to reduce visibility too much during games.

It was amazing how resilient these hockey players were when they adjusted to the new norms and played through it, despite the difficulties the global pandemics presented to them. It was also inspiring how people came together to make sure everyone remained safe, but at the same time still able to play hockey. Hockey is a sport most kids pick up and stick with from a very young age. Families dedicate a crazy amount of time and resources to supporting their young athletes play, and it was good to see them finish their seasons.

Superbowl LV was Played in Full Stadium in Tampa Bay

In the NFL, the league and the union went through a lot of the same headaches as the rest of the professional sports leagues. They may have handled the whole situation better than any other league. After initial conversations about what should be done with the season, the league and the players union came to an agreement to play on Jul 24 and started training camp a few days later.

The NFL was determined to play their whole schedule of games, which would include daily testing and strict protocols. A lot of routine off-the-field behavior was restricted: no visiting indoor nightclubs, big parties, indoor concerts or group dinners. But one thing the NFL wouldn't have would be a bubble. Whereas the NBA was able to send all of their playoff teams to Orlando to live and play on a campus, the roster size and amount of organizational support needed to keep all 32 teams housed and playing in one central location for 5 months while the season played out wasn't considered.

Starting in training camp, every player tested daily, including their off day, and bye weeks and game days. The cost of the testing was reported to near $100 million, which the 32 teams paid for.

The league knew some players would miss games, but the goal was to isolate them, do contact tracing, and keep the season on track. Players were allowed to opt out of the season, essentially freezing their contract and taking a year off. In the end, 67 players chose that options.

The league's ambitious goal was to play all 256 regular season games over the normal 17 weeks, with an extra week of wiggle room available just in case. If there was a significant surge of cases or if anything new came along that caused them to miss a large quantity of games, they could push back the playoffs and Super Bowl to allow for re-scheduling games.

Every stadium's fan policy was governed by the local municipality's policies. 12 stadiums didn't allow fans, while the others limited the crowd to at most 30% capacity. The Dallas Cowboys had an average of approximately 28,000 fans in their 100,000-seat stadium, which was the highest percentage in the league. NFL protocols for the regular season required that the closest rows to the field be blocked with tarps to reduce spectator proximity to the field.

On Oct. 23 the NFL revised their protocol to say if coaches or players had close contact with someone else who tested positive, they had to quarantine for five days. This made it quite a bit more challenging. The New Orleans Saints played a game without any running backs, the Cleveland Browns played a game without any of their core wide receivers available, and the Denver Broncos were forced to play without any of their quarterbacks, when that position group had an infection and all the other quarterbacks on roster had a close contact interaction with an infected player. In the end, 22 games had to be moved from their original day or time, but no games were canceled, a logistical feat that was quite impressive.

Just as planned, the playoffs were held on schedule. One casualty of the protocols was the Cleveland Browns' rookie Head Coach, Kevin Stefanski, He was forced to take in his team's 48-37 Wild Card round victory over the Pittsburgh Steelers from his home, due to a positive test. It was the team's first playoff victory since 1994, and they went on to lose to the eventual runner-up Kansas City Chiefs in the Divisional Playoffs the next week. Stefanski won the Coach of the Year award after the season. So, a little silver lining for the Browns.

Back in March 2020, Tom Brady left the New England Patriots and signed with the Tampa Bay Buccaneers. It was fitting that Tampa Bay was hosting the Super Bowl and for the first time ever, the host city's team made it, taking on the Kansas City Chiefs. They would go on to clobber the Chiefs 31-9, which was Brady's record 7th Super Bowl victory.

There were 24,835 socially distanced fans in attendance for the Super Bowl in Tampa Bay, 7,500 who were healthcare workers invited by the NFL as guests. The league also sold 30,000 cardboard cutouts to fans, to fill in the empty seats. It was quite the tightrope act by the country's most popular league, and people were very excited to have a Super Bowl to watch.

Religion

Churches Served Communion in Individual Plastic Cups

During Holy Communion service, Catholics re-enact the last meal Jesus shared with his disciples by eating a piece of bread and drinking a bit of wine or grape juice. It is meant to be a reflective moment in the life of a believer of Christ. Parishioners make their way to the front of the church and take a drink from a communal chalice handed to them by the officiant.

Other denominations across the country have decided that the best way to deliver the Eucharist of Christ, especially during the pandemic, was to serve them in single serving plastic cups that combine the wine and bread in one. It looked like a single serving coffee creamer with a little cracker underneath. Churchgoers would grab their pillow pack on the way in and when the officiant gave the word, the Communicants would consume the elements. It was deemed more sanitary, and less risky for transmission.

For some denominations, this way worked for the church and the church members alike. But this didn't sit well with the Catholics.

In the Midwest, a church got in trouble for leaving the Eucharist in single serving to-go bags outside the service. They were left spread out on a table for the members to take with them on their way out.

The United States Conference of Catholic Bishops released a statement that said:

> "Distribution of the Eucharist in another vessel or container (a plastic bag, paper cup or a metal pyx) is not warranted. From a public health perspective packaging the Eucharist may even increase risk: CDC guidance suggests that the virus is not easily transmitted by food, whereas passing other containers from person to person involves more contact with surfaces."

Cardinal Robert Sarah from the Vatican denounced the practice of to-go Eucharist as "total madness":

> "God deserves respect; you can't put Him in a bag. I don't know who thought of this absurdity."

Church Services Were Canceled
for Christmas

In 2020, the coronavirus pandemic forced Americans to rethink their traditional Christmas celebrations. Depending on the state or municipality, many churches were closed. So, instead of the usual pageants, carols, and midnight masses, people had to fill out fast-filling attendance registration forms ensuring they could attend a limited service, or they were firing up the laptop to participate in services offered on demand.

While attendance limits for in-person services varied from place to place, some braved the new world and attended church on Christmas Eve and Christmas Day. Other church leaders urged Christians to stay away from gatherings to reduce the spread of the virus. The lack of social interaction and the inability to participate in traditional celebrations lead to loneliness and isolation during the holiday season for some, as travel restrictions and quarantine requirements made it difficult or impossible to see loved ones in person.

Virtual events, such as online concerts and church services, helped people feel more connected to their communities, even if they couldn't gather in person. Some churches organized virtual gatherings, where they can share a meal or exchange gifts over video chat. This was especially important for the members of the church who were isolated.

The lack of a regular Christmas routine and the powerful need for positive news given the special circumstances, had many Americans pouring new energy into making the holiday uplifting, while still maintaining social distancing guidelines. Christmas trees and decorations were up earlier than usual, partly because people were just at home more, and had less to do.

Some people experienced that those around them reflected on the season's meaning in a new way. That Christmas was a powerful time of a very trying year, and many used it as an opportunity to count their blessings. Make no mistake, Christmas would come whether there was a pandemic or not—and people were looking for something to celebrate. That Christmas brought hope, joy, and new life, when most people needed that most in their lives.

Car Church Services Became
Extremely Popular

The sun shone in the sky on a bright Sunday morning. The birds were chirping, and the flowers were blooming; it seemed as if everything in nature was perfectly normal. Meanwhile, something strange was happening in churches all across the country.

It started when people became aware of the dangers posed by COVID-19 and began to become more cautious in their daily lives. Suddenly, churches, which usually held their services in beautiful chapels made to worship God, were forced to think of alternative ways to provide spiritual guidance for their congregations.

The solution for many churches came easily: outdoor Sunday service from the comfort of one's own vehicle. Churches began setting up large parking lots with rows of parked cars. Once everyone arrived and got settled in, a loud P.A. system, or in many cases a special radio frequency that could be tuned into from one's car, broadcasted the Good Word.

This created some interesting scenarios. On one hand, it provided an opportunity for people who may not otherwise feel comfortable attending church services to still hear the gospel preached. For others, who love the feeling of attending church, but may not love the social interactions of church (peace-be-with-you handshakes, passing the donation plates), they could still listen without having to leave their vehicles. Plenty of parishioners got to attend a church service without the trappings of church—a feat long dreamt about, but never achievable, before COVID-19 came along.

On the other hand, it caused a sense of disconnection between members of the congregation – there was no way for them to mingle or discuss points brought up during sermons as they normally would do after services indoors. The sense of community was generally lost. Even if members were near the congregation, many still felt apart.

The car church idea continued with these innovative measures until life returned to normal again, after COVID-19 eased its grip on society at large. For some it was exactly what was needed: to maintain some level of consistency throughout the experience.

Funeral Services Strictly Limited Number of Allowed Attendees

The COVID-19 pandemic had a devastating effect on the funeral service industry, forcing people to mourn their loved ones in isolation and make do with video calls instead of gathering in person. Across the country, each state and sometimes county and city enacted different restrictions to help contain the spread of the virus. Most places also mandated social distancing protocols such as wearing masks and always maintaining six feet of distance between individuals. Some states went so far as to prohibit singing at funerals.

Take New York State as an example: Governor Andrew Cuomo issued an executive order back in March 2020 that limited funerals to no more than 50 mourners while imposing strict social distancing measures such as six feet between attendees and mandatory face masks. In addition, churches were required to livestream any service that exceeded that number of attendees for families who could not attend physically to still be able to pay their respects remotely. Iowa, as well as many other states, limited funerals to 10 people or less with social distancing measures enforced. Meanwhile, Texas allowed up to 100 guests with similar safety protocols encouraged but not mandated.

The attendance limitation was the most devastating aspect for those who experienced the loss of a loved one during the pandemic. The reality that there couldn't be a large service with extended family and friends to lend their support was especially disheartening. Services that would normally bring dozens or even hundreds of individuals together to pay tribute to a beloved individual were limited to an incredibly small number. It weighed heavy on those who were mourning during these times of uncertainty and distress.

The purpose of the memorial service is to honor and remember the deceased while offering comfort and solace to those in grief. Since the beginning of humanity, the way we put our deceased to rest is very important to the survivors. With such few people present, ceremonies were still conducted in meaningful ways, but it really robbed the surviving friends and family of part of the grieving process. That part of the person's lifetime is always going to feel weird or unnatural, and that is just so unfortunate.

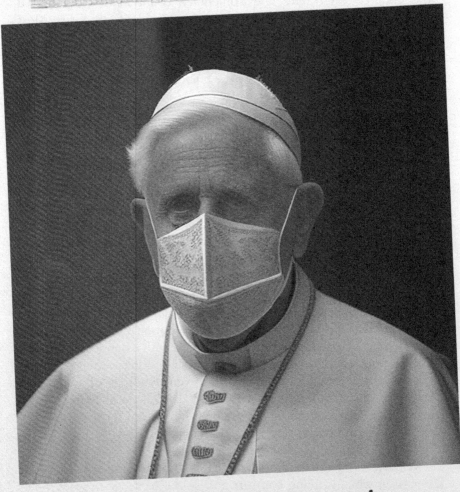

The Catholic Church
Issued Guidance During
the Pandemic

The COVID-19 pandemic presented unprecedented challenges to the Catholic Church, as it did to many other religious organizations around the world. In response to the spread of the virus, the Church quickly adapted and found ways to continue its mission of spreading the Gospel and serving its members and the wider community.

One of the first and most visible changes for many Catholics was the suspension of in-person Masses and other services. As governments implemented measures to slow the spread of the virus, including lockdowns and social distancing rules, many churches were forced to close their doors to the public. This was a difficult decision for many priests and bishops, as the celebration of Mass is a central part of Catholic life and is believed to be a source of grace and spiritual nourishment.

To continue to minister to their flocks, many churches turned to online platforms such as Zoom and YouTube to stream Masses and other events. Some priests and bishops also began to record their own homilies and prayers and share them on social media, to reach Catholics who were unable to attend Mass in person.

The Vatican issued guidance to Catholics on how to observe their faith during the pandemic. This included recommendations on the usage of face masks and the suspension of certain rituals, such as the sharing of the Communion cup, to reduce the risk of transmission. The Vatican also encouraged Catholics to pray for those affected by the virus and to offer support to those in need, particularly to those who were isolated or facing financial hardship. Later, they issued guidance to Catholics that it is morally acceptable to use COVID-19 vaccines.

In addition to adapting to the challenges of the pandemic, the Catholic Church also played an active role in aiding those affected by COVID-19. Many Catholic charities and organizations, such as Catholic Relief Services and Caritas, were involved in the distribution of food and other essentials to those in need, both in the United States and around the world. In some cases, churches and other Catholic organizations also served as vaccination sites or provided other medical assistance.

People Virtually Attended Church Services Via Online Streaming

When the pandemic hit, many churches had to figure out alternative ways to keep their congregations connected with one another. As restrictions began to be implemented, it quickly became clear that in-person worship services were no longer a viable option. It was at this point that churches started looking for creative solutions to keep their members spiritually connected.

One of the most unique ideas among religious institutions was to offer virtual services online. This was something completely new and completely unexpected for many churchgoers, who had grown accustomed to meeting in person each week for mass or other ceremonies. It was a strange concept–being able to attend religious services from the comfort of their homes instead of in physical churches or temples. Spiritual fulfillment without changing out of your pajamas was now an option!

To make these virtual services possible, many churches had to make big changes in terms of technology and infrastructure. Internet connections had to be improved, websites needed building and maintaining, and video conferencing apps had to be used so that everyone could join together virtually. Of course, some people found this whole process confusing and baffling, and churches had to scramble and lean on congregation members for help.

The lack of physicality posed a challenge and mental hurdle for those attending online services – how could they feel connected when they weren't physically present? Despite all these struggles, it soon became apparent that virtual worship services were quite popular amongst many congregations. People found comfort in being able to still connect with others during such uncertain times by attending online masses and prayers from their own homes.

In addition to virtual worship services, many churches also made use of social media outlets such as Facebook and Instagram in order to stay connected with members outside of live service times. Often there would be posts from pastors offering words of encouragement or prayer requests along with Bible verses or inspirational quotes; as well as pictures or videos showcasing various ministries within the church community. These posts gave congregation members a chance to stay engaged even if they weren't available for live streaming or video conferencing at any given time throughout the week.

Also, raising funds had to move to the digital world. Churches rely on donations from the congregation to pay bills and fund the ministries of the church. A good portion of these funds are raised with collection plates during services, and without a physical service, many churches had to go to 100% digital fund transfers via the same platforms airing the worship services.

It was an interesting and trying time for those involved in religious organizations, forced into virtual church services. For many, it became a way to expand their presence. In the long run, it was a positive opportunity for their churches, opening their doors to people who may not have otherwise been able to attend due to geographical or physical restraints. For those faithful individuals who sought solace through prayer and faith while living through an unprecedented global health crisis, online church was a welcomed way of providing spiritual guidance while still adhering to social distancing protocols.

Travel

Airlines Stopped Selling Middle Seats on Flights

COVID-19 struck a huge blow to travel plans. Vacations were scrapped or postponed as families made the choice to stay at home and business travel plans were canceled as companies chose to keep their employees safe. People were rightfully concerned about the virus spreading and being in close contact with strangers on planes.

As a result, USA airlines took a huge hit in 2020--over $35 billion in lost revenues. Most airlines cut their routes and parked a lot of their aircraft. Many flew routes at 10-20% of the airplane's capacity.

In the early stages of the pandemic, the 11 biggest United States airlines (Alaska Airlines, Allegiant, American, Delta, Frontier, Hawaiian Airlines, JetBlue, Southwest, Spirit, Sun Country, and United) either blocked middle seats or limited the number of tickets sold, or both, to make sure flights weren't completely full.

This was quite easy to implement when travel demand was so low. They didn't have the demand to fill up a plane, so it was easy to follow a mandate to leave the middle seats unsold and empty on flights.

The 6-foot social distancing rules from the ground went away on an airplane. In a 3-by-3 seat configuration, having a middle seat empty at best gets you a couple of feet of distance. The policies were a combination of psychology for making flyers feel safer, and a product of the airlines unable to completely fill up a flight.

Of the non-discount carriers, American Airlines was the first airline to announce that they would begin re-selling flights to 100% capacity, starting July 1, 2020. Slowly, as demand started to increase, the rest of the airlines followed suit and relaxed their rules about leaving middle seats empty. Delta Airlines was the last holdout. They had positioned themselves as the "safe" airline, holding to their policy of keeping middle seats open longer than any other airline.

After the levels of travel returned to near pre-pandemic levels, one holdover from the seat blocking era remained. There was a new way to make sure the middle seat would be left empty: most carriers allowed travelers to also book the seat next to theirs as well, to ensure it would remain empty. For the full ticket price, of course.

In-flight Food and Beverage
Service Stopped

The COVID-19 pandemic had a devastating impact on the airline industry. They scrambled like every other industry to stay in business while at the same time keeping their employees and customers safe. To that end, they put several policies in place. Some were clearly great ideas and made a lot of sense, and some of them seemed...well, silly.

To comply with social distancing guidelines during the coronavirus pandemic, major U.S. airlines implemented measures to restrict food and beverage offerings for most passengers on domestic flights. In fact, on most flights, including longer trips, many carriers ceased providing alcoholic beverages altogether. The airlines claimed that these measures, which were mostly implemented in March or April, helped their employees and passengers follow social distancing protocols, as it minimized their contact with each other.

Except, the rule didn't always apply to the whole plane.

For instance, American Airlines suspended its alcohol service in the main cabin on domestic flights. However, passengers seated in first class and those flying on long-haul international flights could still request wine and cocktails. Also, in first class, customers could access bottled water and Biscoff cookies or pretzels. The airline said that the policy aimed to minimize interactions between flight attendants and customers.

So, one could deduce that interactions with customers in first class, or international travelers, was somehow safer than interactions with the main cabin.

But, a more cynical person might have guessed that first- and business-class passengers only accounted for about 5% of all passenger traffic, but generated approximately 30% of all passenger revenues, according to the International Air Transport Association. These passengers were the lifeblood of air travel, and as such, airlines were very protective of them. Keeping these high-paying customers happy trumped the "safety measures" that flight staffs followed for the rest of the passengers, who also happened to love eating Biscoff cookies and drinking alcoholic beverages on airplanes.

Passengers Were Required to Wear Masks Except When Eating or Drinking

All airlines implemented a mask wearing policy on their flights. It was one of the most unusual and annoying restrictions that many of us had to endure while traveling. Most people politely obliged, whether they agreed with the policy or the efficacy of the rule in the first place. They had somewhere to get to, and the only real way to get there was on an airplane. Some had complete meltdowns. Just search "refusing to wear mask on plane" on YouTube and get your popcorn ready. (Some people lost their damn minds during the pandemic--this is just a fact.)

The risk of catching COVID-19 while on an airplane was thought to be minimal due to the high quality of air supplied in the cabin, which surpasses that of most indoor settings. Passengers faced the same direction, and the seats acted as natural barriers. The air flowed from top to bottom and was refreshed 20-30 times an hour with a combination of HEPA-filtered and fresh air from outside. 99.93% of the bacteria/viruses were eliminated in the filtering process. Yet, the airlines required passengers to wear masks. Many questioned that.

Although the airlines stopped food and drink service on airplanes, most of them still encouraged passengers to bring their own beverages and snacks on board. Those skeptical of the mask policy had their argument bolstered when the airlines created an exception to their own rule: Passengers may pull their masks down while eating or drinking on the plane. Coronavirus apparently couldn't spread while someone snacked. This was just pure science.

Despite the annoyance factor, there was a certain level of absurdity to the whole thing that made it almost comical. For the defiant few, the game was to slow-play their eating and drinking. If they could eat their bag of Doritos and drink their bottle of water at a slow enough pace, they could justify having their mask down for the entire flight!

The flight attendants' job was that of a hall monitor. Pacing up and down the aisle, keeping an internal clock going on each passenger's mask. If a passenger went two or three minutes with their mask down to their chin, it was a quick "Excuse me, ma'am, can you please put your mask on?". This cat and mouse game turned into a sport, and helped pass the time of even the longest flights.

Uber Required Masks and Stopped Allowing Front Seat Passengers

During the height of the pandemic, people stopped going out. Most businesses were shut down and the amounts of get-togethers dropped. People weren't commuting into their office jobs. And a lot of air travel was put on hold. Accordingly, the need to rely on a rideshare service plummeted.

In fact, at the worst point in April 2020, demand for Uber rides was down 80% from the previous year. The company cut 3,700 corporate jobs and their million or so drivers were deeply affected by the loss of income and health risks of remaining behind the wheel.

By June, things were starting to loosen up a bit and the ride sharing business began to rebound some. The demand was only down 70% from the previous year. Uber found themselves facing a unique set of challenges to keep their passengers and their drivers safe.

They were the leaders in their industry to roll out new pandemic related policies. The company implemented a mandatory mask rule for both drivers and passengers and had facial scanning technology to make sure that their drivers were complying. They shipped $50 million worth of masks, disinfectant spray, and bleach wipes to their drivers, to ensure their passengers had a safe and sanitized ride.

But perhaps the most significant change was the no sitting in the front seat rule. To maintain a safe distance between driver and passengers, Uber implemented a policy that required all passengers to sit in the backseat. This meant that the coveted front seat, which many enjoy for its extra legroom and better view, was off-limits. It also meant that parties greater than three had to hail two separate vehicles. Four tends to be a magic number--plenty of double dates or nights out in a group start with that exact amount of people. Now, those four people were going to have to double their rides, which also happened to double the volume of fares, and the underlying revenue, for Uber.

Some Uber drivers were afraid that the company would cut off their partnership if the drivers refused to pick up unmasked passengers. Uber stood behind their drivers and said that drivers were well within their rights to demand passengers to wear masks, and that they would kick any users off the platform who refused to comply with the rule.

Beaches Were Shut Down

All throughout the pandemic, being outside was better at stopping the spread of the virus than being inside. Between the combination of the wind and the sun, transmission rates were measurably reduced when people were sprung out of their houses and enjoyed the outdoors.

One of the best places to enjoy being outdoors is the beach, in the middle of the summer. Beautiful, sunny, cloud-free skies, warm salty sea breeze air, and delightful sounds of splashing waves and dozens of people running, swimming, and building epic sandcastles greets you at the beach. Most people famously find the beach relaxing and delightful.

But, during the summer of 2020, the beach was anything but delightful. It became sort of an apocalyptic sandbox, full of rules. From the Los Angeles County's website, from July of 2020:

> The beach is OPEN for active recreational use, such as launching watercraft from, and subject to additional health & safety rules & restrictions. However, the following amenities all remain CLOSED until further notice:
>
> • Walkway
> • Parking Lot
> • Picnic Tables & Shelters
> • BBQ Grills
> • Playground
> • All beach volleyball courts have had their nets removed

One of the best peaceful, relaxing, leisurely ways to spend a sunny day outside of the home, was effectively reduced to a mini prison: not being able to park, not being able to play, not having a place to prepare or gather to eat food, and absolutely no volleyball. Beaches roped off the courts and even bulldozed huge sand mounds on top of the courts so people wouldn't get any funny idea and sneak up their own makeshift nets.

In one of the most dumfounding decisions to come from the COVID-19 response, many overzealous municipalities gave a new definition to the phrase "Life's a Beach!"

Camper and RV Dealers Completely Sold Out Their Inventories

The coronavirus pandemic brought on a huge surge in the recreational vehicle (RV) and camper industry. Many travelers either canceled or delayed their prior vacation plans. The airline industry had all sorts of restrictions, and some people didn't want to be on cross-country flights with hundreds of other people in close quarters. Also, many popular vacation destinations were shut down, so people turned to the great outdoors.

The appeal of the RV was that the whole family that was already staying at home together, could hit the road together, in their own little vacation bubble. People who were cooped up and wanted to get out of their houses could hit the open road. The RV was the solution to their problems.

Suddenly, everyone wanted to hit the road, and what better way to do that than by purchasing a giant metal house on wheels?

In a normal year, only about 25% of all RV and camper sales are attributed to first-time buyers. The rest are repeat buyers, who typically will trade in a previous model when they make their new purchase. During the pandemic, as high as 80% of sales were first-time buyers, who obviously didn't have anything to trade in. The result was a lot of camper and RV sales lots sat empty by the end of summer 2020, and demand for any type of vehicle soared. Reservations at campgrounds also skyrocketed, and getting a spot proved difficult.

Of course, it wasn't just the pandemic-induced cabin fever that fueled this sudden interest in campers and RVs. It was also the government stimulus checks. Suddenly, people had money burning a hole in their pockets and what better way to spend it than on a giant metal house on wheels? It was like paying for a cross-country vacation, and the biggest souvenir gets parked next to the garage when you return home.

Taking a camper or RV vacation was a way for families to break the monotony of spending all their time cooped up inside their house. They created a positive experience and stayed together in an otherwise bleak time. Everyone was keeping themselves safe and practicing social distancing. They just wanted to do it with a little change of scenery.

Cruise Ship Passengers Were Held in Quarantine for Two Weeks

At the beginning of the pandemic, people were stuck home and a ton of businesses were shutting down. People needed fresh air and exercise and were looking for ways to support social distancing as the coronavirus spread across the United States. One of the best ways to do this was to take advantage of the United States' most treasured assets, our National Parks.

On March 18, 2020, the Secretary of the Interior David Bernhardt sent out a directive to the National Park Service to waive entrance fees of parks that remained open. "This small step makes it a little easier for the American public to enjoy the outdoors in our incredible National Parks," he said. This was a very noble reaction by a government official to reduce the barriers for citizens to visit the beautiful parks. However, the good feeling didn't last long.

The CDC and state and local public health official applied pressure, and soon enough, the National Park Service changed their policy and operations at many parks. Most of the public buildings, including visitor centers and bathroom facilities, were completely shut down. There are 62 national parks operated by the National Park Service, and most of them were highly impacted and experienced closures of some sort.

Of the most popular national parks, the level of disruption varied. Some were completely shut down. Some were accessible but all core services such as restrooms, campgrounds, visitor centers and main trails were shut down. In short, even if the park had areas that were "open", it wasn't a welcoming environment.

The biggest problem with shutting down services within the National Parks while still allowing visitors, was the waste left behind. The National Park Services has always urged visitors to practice Leave No Trace principles—like pack-in and pack-out—to keep the parks clean and safe for everyone. Many people went to the parks and used the areas where they could, but many visitors didn't practice these guidelines. Without facilities open, and lack of services to collect waste and monitor regulations, many of the National Parks were left with litter, human waste, and graffiti, which polluted our nation's gems. Unfortunately, this was not a great look for our country's citizens.

State and National Parks Were
Closed Down

In February 2020, the captain of the cruise ship *Diamond Princess* was informed that a disembarked passenger tested positive for the COVID-19 virus. The captain received that information and took no action. Meanwhile, the ship's crew kept the big floating party going!

Two days later, at 11:00 pm, the captain spoke to the whole ship. He announced that everyone must remain in their cabins. The ship was docked at Yokohama Port in Japan to wait for health officials to administer tests and discuss symptoms with the passengers aboard. Soon, they found out that they had the largest concentrated number of active COVID-19 cases on the planet aboard (outside mainland China). The first positive cases were found on February 5th. Thus began the infamous "Diamond Princess Quarantine".

As days went by and the quarantine continued, the passengers and crew seemed to lack understanding about the severity of the virus. The ship's normal crew had to handle the passengers themselves. There was no Special Ops Covid Team to swoop in and run this mission. There was a shortage of personal protective equipment (PPE) for the crew. They did face-to-face deliveries to each passenger cabin for each of the three meals per day, but re-use the same gloves for each delivery. The testing on the ship was reserved for those who started to experience flu-like symptoms. However, nearly 18% of cases on the ship were found among asymptomatic passengers, as the virus was spread unnoticed. A total of 712 cases of COVID-19 were confirmed on the ship.

The Diamond Princess quarantine served as a warning to the rest of the world about the severity of the COVID-19 pandemic and the need for effective measures to control its spread. It also highlighted the importance of clear communication, adequate supply of PPE, and comprehensive testing to combat the virus.

Following 39 days on board the ship (including more than three weeks in quarantine), the final group of 2,666 passengers ultimately disembarked and commenced their journeys home on February 27th. However, they had to then begin another two-week quarantine in their home countries, which essentially reset the clock. Then, after those two weeks, they finally got to go home, just into time to join the experience of the rest of the world falling apart from the pandemic. It would be really easy to say those passengers will probably never go on another cruise, but you never know. People who love cruises really love cruises.

Disneyland Was Closed Down While Disney World Stayed Open

Once upon a time, in the land of COVID-19, Disneyland in California found itself in a bit of a pickle. The park, known for its magical adventures and childhood joy, was forced to close its doors due to a pesky little virus making its way around the world.

But a little over two thousand miles away, in the Sunshine State of Florida, another Disney theme park was still very much open for business. Disney World, the larger and more extravagant of the two parks, was fully operational. How could this be?

To understand, this tale began months earlier, in March of 2020. As things started to shut down across the country, both family vacation destinations closed their doors within a couple of days of each other. But after a few weeks, each state's leadership took drastically different approaches towards reopening their state's vast tourist attractions.

Florida's benchmarks for reopening businesses, parks, and other facilities echoed the White House's 'Reopening America' guidelines, if somewhat less strict. Florida began a "phase two" reopening in early June and Disney went to work crafting reopening plans for their Florida parks.

Guests and employees were required to wear masks and undergo temperature checks. Parades, fireworks, and other big crowd activities were paused. Disney would encourage contactless payment systems and expand its existing mobile order systems in restaurants. Restrictions were placed on the number of guests, and they would be required to reserve their park passes ahead of time.

Governor Ron DeSantis, a Republican, had a staunch belief about not shutting down Florida's economy again, and he approved Disney World's reopening plans for July 11, 2020.

Meanwhile, California handled reopening their own tourist attractions in a completely different manner. Governor Gavin Newsom, a Democrat, was not as eager to get his state back to normal. They locked down businesses much more aggressively than Florida, or almost any other state in the union. Disneyland and other California theme parks remained closed while they awaited long-promised reopening guidelines from the state's leaders. In October, Newsom sent health officials to The Sunshine State to inspect the protocols in place at Disney World.

Newsom said, "I want folks to come back and tell me what they saw, what their own experience was. Because this is serious."

Well, either the envoy must have seen something they didn't like, or Governor Newxom really went on a power trip, because theme parks remained locked down for the rest of 2020. In fact, they were among the last businesses allowed to reopen in California in April 2021, 13 months after they closed.

When they finally reopened, they did so following most of the same protocols put in place in Florida months earlier. Capacity was capped at 25%, reservations were required, hugs and handshakes with Mickey and other characters were strictly off limits, and the famous parades and fireworks shows were shelved to limit crowding. Initially, it was only opened to California residents or out-of-state residents with full vaccination records.

In the end, the story of closing and opening Disney theme parks was a tale of two very distinct lands, lead by two very different rulers, each with very separate agendas. To determine which ruler was the hero and which was the villain will be left to each reader's own imagination. It would be very lovely if we could close this chapter with the standard "…and they both lived happily ever after" ending. Very lovely, indeed.

Entertainment

Late Night Show Hosts
Broadcasted Their Shows
from Their Own Homes

With everyone stuck at home, late-night talk show hosts, used to performing in front of a live studio audience, were faced with a dilemma: how to keep the show going, while also keeping themselves and their crew safe? The solution was to bring the show to their own homes.

Jimmy Fallon, Jimmy Kimmel, Seth Meyers, Conan O'Brien, and others got creative, setting up makeshift studios in their living rooms, kitchens, and basements, and using technology to connect with their guests and audiences. It wasn't always smooth sailing—there were technical glitches, jokes and bits that absolutely bombed, and awkward production moments as they figured out the best way to fill an hour of semi-scripted television programming from their homes, but they eventually found their footing, and put out an entertaining product.

One of the biggest challenges was finding ways to keep their shows fresh and engaging, despite the limited scope of their surroundings and without all their production staff. They got creative. They found new ways to do sketches and segments that worked within the confines of their homes. Their kids helped with the on-screen graphics. Their wives would double as their co-hosts. They had virtual appearances by celebrities, sharing jokes and stories, and offering a glimpse into their own quarantined lives. They had DIY segments demonstrating how to make everything from cocktails to papier mache masks, using only household items and a dash of humor and improvisation. They navigated the challenges and the uncertainty of the times and used their platforms to offer comfort, levity, and perspective.

The hosts addressed the weighty issues of the day, from the pandemic, to the social protests, to the turbulent political landscape, with honesty, humor, and humanity. It was a time when they let you behind the facade and presented themselves as real human beings, and it was very touching.

For many viewers, the late night talk show was a source of solace and connection during a time of isolation and anxiety. It offered a respite from the chaos and the uncertainty of the world. It was a reminder that, even in the darkest of times, there is always the possibility of laughter and joy. It probably made some television executives wonder if they needed such gigantic staffs for these shows once they returned to normal.

Local News Broadcasts Had On-Air Talent Working Remotely

For operations that routinely tackled vicious crimes, inspiring community leaders, dangerous weather conditions, and heartbreaking sports stories, the coronavirus outbreak presented unfamiliar territory for the local news industry. The TV newsroom is typically bustling with writers, reporters, and producers working in close quarters, but the virus turned these into eerily quiet spaces due to social distancing measures.

Journalists had to adapt by working remotely, conducting interviews using extended microphones, and focusing on stories closer to their homes. They attended almost daily press conferences with governors and mayors giving up-to-the-minute updates on their pandemic responses. Rather than traveling together in news vans, reporters and crews went to stories separately.

Fewer people and technicians were asked to work in the studios and newsrooms to mind social distancing guidelines. Makeup and hair professionals started wearing masks and gloves when preparing anchors for the camera. Reporters had the option to decline an assignment if they felt it was unsafe.

Meteorologists and sports anchors started delivering their reports from their respective living rooms. Some stations had their anchors do the full news broadcast from home. It was sometimes a train wreck, but other times it worked surprisingly well, which was a testament to great production staffs and highly professional on-air talent. Some of the criticism of news—that it's just robots reading teleprompters—went out the window when the personalities and realness of the people responsible for reporting the news came out.

The humorous element will be what endured from the pandemic era newscast. Everyday home situations played out in the background, while a frantic newscaster tried not to break on camera. The internet is full of clips like a mischievous cat knocking over a vase on the bookshelf, or a toddler running into the room asking if Daddy can play ('Sure, Buddy, give Daddy just a minute, I'm doing the weather forecast for the half the state of Utah here."). Those moments brought some brevity into the homes of the viewers during an otherwise hectic news period.

'Tiger King' Was the Biggest
Pop Culture Phenomenon

One thing that was a bummer during COVID-19 was the lack of new content available to watch on cable, streaming platforms, and theaters.

There were more new shows than ever, with something for everyone's taste, but, the second week of March 2020, across the board, all television productions shut down. In the world of tight turnarounds and very little time dedicated to keeping shows "in the can" (completely done with production and ready to air), it was a matter of time before networks and streamers ran out of new fresh content.

Netflix was ready for this challenge. In fact, as people began to stay home during the pandemic, Netflix thrived. In the first three months of 2020, nearly 16 million users created accounts, which was almost double the number that signed up in the last few months of 2019.

The crown jewel of the pandemic lockdown period was The Tiger King. It was released on March 20, just as many Americans were settling into their new routine of not leaving their homes. In the first week of its release, it attracted (according to Nielsen) an estimated 34.3 million viewers. That is comparable to how many viewers Laverne & Shirley, Happy Days, and All in the Family pulled in during the 70s, when there were only three lousy channels to pick from.

You could not escape Tiger King talk. It was a true crime documentary miniseries which told the story of Joe Exotic and Carole Baskin, the former an owner of a big cat private zoo, and the latter an animal rights activist who tried to take him down.

It was discussed on Zoom Happy Hours, around socially distanced bonfires, and was the fodder of all the late-night shows recording from their hosts' homes. People loved debating what really happened and loved discussing the crazy characters. Even months later, by Halloween, it remained one of the most popular costumes.

For the people that stayed home and went into binge mode, those first weeks of the pandemic and Tiger King will forever be linked.

Netflix Held Back Season Three of 'Ozark'

For fans of the hit Netflix show *Ozark*, the anticipation was palpable, as they eagerly awaited the release of the highly anticipated third season. However, as the pandemic raged on, there was a growing sense of uncertainty about when the new season would be able to debut.

For the creators of *Ozark*, the pandemic presented a unique set of challenges. Like many other productions, the show had to halt filming in the early stages of the pandemic, and it was unclear when it would be safe to resume. In the meantime, the writers, producers, and actors had to find ways to stay connected and creative, despite being physically separated.

Despite the setbacks, the team behind *Ozark* remained committed to delivering the best season possible. They worked tirelessly to finish filming, using innovative techniques and protocols to ensure the safety of their cast and crew. They also spent countless hours in post-production, polishing and perfecting the episodes to meet the high standards of their fans.

As the release date approached, there were rumors and speculation about whether the show would be able to debut on time. Some fans speculated that the show would be released early, to provide some much-needed entertainment and distraction during the pandemic. Others speculated that the release date would be pushed back, as the pandemic continued to disrupt production and release schedules.

In the end, the team behind *Ozark* made the decision to stick with their original release date. They released the third season in full, on the same day and time that it had originally been planned.

For fans of the show, the wait was worth it. The third season of *Ozark* was met with widespread acclaim, with critics praising its tight plot, compelling performances, and timely themes. The show's popularity seemed to grow during the pandemic, as more and more people tuned in to escape the stresses and monotony of everyday life.

Although everyone would have welcomed it a month or two sooner, the third season of *Ozark* provided a much-needed escape and distraction, at a time when it was needed the most.

Movie Theaters
Closed Down

For movie lovers, the pandemic presented a unique challenge: how to satisfy their cravings for the big screen, when the big screen was no longer an option? As the pandemic spread and governments implemented lockdown measures, movie theaters around the world were forced to close their doors. It was a devastating blow for an industry that was already struggling to adapt to the changing landscape of entertainment.

For many movie theaters, the closure was a death knell. Faced with mounting expenses and no income, they were forced to shut their doors permanently. Some theaters invested in technology to enable drive-in screenings, allowing audiences to watch films from the safety of their own cars.

Despite these efforts, the closure of movie theaters had a ripple effect on the entire film industry. Studios were forced to delay the release of their blockbuster films and independent filmmakers struggled to get their work seen. Film festivals were postponed or canceled and filmmakers lost the opportunity to showcase their work to a wider audience.

For movie fans, the closure of theaters was a difficult pill to swallow. They missed the shared experience of watching a film on the big screen, the thrill of seeing the latest blockbuster with a crowd, and the sense of community that came from attending a movie with friends or loved ones.

As the pandemic began to recede and theaters slowly reopened, movie fans were able to return to the big screen. They returned with a renewed appreciation for the magic and power of film and a determination to support their local theaters and the artists who brought their stories to life.

In the end, the closure of movie theaters was a difficult and challenging experience, but it also proved that the love of film is resilient and enduring. It reminded us of the power of storytelling, the importance of community, and the enduring appeal of the big screen experience.

Top Gun: Maverick Premier Was
Delayed 2 Years

The original *Top Gun* was released in 1986. A young Tom Cruise starred as Maverick, pushing his way through the Navy's top school for fighter pilots. With the young star power, high flying action sequences, and epic soundtrack, it was one of the most beloved movies of the 80's.

For 35 years, audiences awaited a sequel. In 2010, Paramount began development and *Top Gun: Maverick* finally began filming in 2018. Tom Cruise and Val Kilmer would reprise their roles, and the hype for the movie was as high as any movie, ever, without exaggeration.

It was initially slated for a summer 2019 release but then was pushed to the summer of 2020 to allow for "production to work out all the complex flight sequences," according to Deadline. Then the pandemic happened.

With everything across the country closing, including most movie theaters, Paramount Pictures made the wise but difficult decision to push the movie's release date back to avoid empty or closed theaters. Other studios decided the best business decision was to release their movies direct to viewer stuck at home, using video-on-demand platforms. *Trolls World Tour*, for instance, made $95 million in three weeks streaming on-demand, which made Universal Pictures happy.

But *Top Gun: Maverick* was not the sort of movie to debut on a small screen. This was the type of movie that needed the full movie theater experience—a big screen with bigger sound and a full auditorium of fans—to enjoy it fully. "I make movies for the big screen," their star Tom Cruise insisted. He didn't want this movie debuting in homes.

After five separate delays and pushbacks, the $152 million sequel was pushed to May 27, 2022, Memorial Day Weekend, finally ready to debut two years after the original date.

As it turned out, Paramount and Tom Cruise made box office gold. The film opened to $160.5 million over the four-day holiday weekend. It went on to top $1 billion worldwide, which went down as Tom Cruise's biggest movie ever. People were ready to return to theaters, especially for this movie which was teased in front of them throughout the entire pandemic.

Tom Hanks Made Covid-19 Seem More Real

On March 12, 2020, one of the most beloved actors on the planet, Tom Hanks, announced that he and his wife, Rita Wilson, had been diagnosed with COVID-19. Hanks was in Australia doing pre-production for the new movie *Elvis*. The star couple contracted the disease at a time when Australia had only 120 confirmed cases. Rita Wilson had performed at the Sydney Opera House the weekend before and did a media appearance on Monday. The couple was responsible and quarantined. By Wednesday, Hanks posted on Instagram:

> "Well, now. What to do next? The Medical Officials have protocols that must be followed. We Hanks' will be tested, observed, and isolated for as long as public health and safety requires. Not much more to it than a one-day-at-a-time approach, no? We'll keep the world posted and updated.
>
> Take care of yourselves!
> Hanx!"

Tom Hanks was the everyman of Hollywood. Movies like *Forrest Gump*, *Cast Away*, *Saving Private Ryan* and *Apollo 13* made him universally loved.

The news spread quickly throughout the world, and it was hard to find someone who hadn't heard of the couple's diagnoses. For many people, a big-name celebrity testing positive for the disease made it seem more real, and highlighted the realities of COVID-19. For the next two weeks the couple kept the public updated on their status via social media. They encouraged others who had the symptoms to go get tested and be smart about self-quarantining.

In those two weeks, a lot of the world's view of COVID-19 shifted and changed dramatically. By March 22, more than 335,000 people had contracted the virus and over 14,641 had died. Employers sent employees home and many found themselves in the same situation the high-profile couple had. Somehow, Tom and Rita established a protocol for what to do when you must stay home and wait out the disease. On that day, Tom and Rita were coming out of quarantine, he posted:

> "This, too, shall pass. We can figure this out."

Celebrities Collaborated on New Version of 'Imagine'

While everyone stayed at home and productions for television and movies shut down, the spotlight was dimmed on celebrities. Six days into her self-quarantine, *Wonder Woman* actress Gal Gadot posted a video montage of fellow high-profile actors and actresses on her Instagram with the following message:

> "Hey, guys. Day 6 in self-quarantine, and I gotta say that these past few days got me feeling a bit philosophical. This virus has affected the entire world—everyone. Doesn't matter who you are or where you're from. We are all in this together. We will get through it together. Let's imagine together. Sing with us. All love to you, from me and my dear friends."

She then kicked off the first line of John Lennon's "Imagine", which then cut to 21 other cameos of celebrities taking a turn at singing a line from the song. It was quirky, unexpected, and quite awful.

While it was sort of a novelty to hear and see some of the world's favorite celebrities take their turns singing a very well-loved song, it came off as a bit tone deaf, both literally and figuratively.

Gadot said in her introduction that she saw a video filmed in Italy of a man playing the trumpet from his balcony. *That* video was organic, unplanned, and truly touching. Her video was contrived and featured Amy Adams, Mark Ruffalo, Will Ferrell, Zoë Kravitz, Kristen Wiig, and Natalie Portman, among others, over-performing a song that is perhaps flawless and never needs to be covered. The song is also about imagining a world without materialism or borders, which is ironic.

The pool of singers included some of the most liberal celebrities in Hollywood. Those ultra-wealthy famous people, in their gorgeous marble kitchens and cavernous living rooms, tried to spread the message that we are all in this together. However, people in the real world, the essential workers, didn't get to hang out and make fun videos with their friends. These people have a bottomless pit for acceptance and crave attention, and this came off as a desperate grab for ours. It was one of the most cringeworthy things that was released during the pandemic, and remains a running joke in America today.

ESPN Ran Out of Live Sports Programming

Rudy Gobert is an NBA player who stands 7'1" and has a 7'9" wingspan. He won back-to-back Defensive Player of the Year awards, and because he hails from France, he earned the nickname "Stifle Tower".

But his role in testing positive for COVID-19 and forcing the league's decision to halt games earned him another nickname: Patient Zero.

On March 11, 2020, the Jazz and Thunder players were on the court, moments away from tip-off, when word broke that Gobert, who was not at the arena due to being ill with flu-like symptoms, had become the league's first positive COVID-19 case, setting into motion a very fast moving chain of events. The league had the court cleared of all players, coaches, and officials faster than Gobert can swat a would-be lay-up into the third row of fans. After a few minutes, the public address announcer told the crowd that the game was canceled. Just moments later, the NBA suspended the season.

This was the first domino to fall in what would be one of the darkest periods for televised sports since they started airing sports on cable.

The next day MLB canceled the remainder of their spring training schedule, and also postponed the start of their regular season, which was scheduled to begin March 26. It eventually resumed on July 23.

The same day, the NHL canceled the remainder of its regular season, and a few months later announced their postseason would start on August 1.

The two biggest crown jewels of springtime sports, college basketball's March Madness tournament, and professional golf's Masters Tournament, were both canceled.

Major League Soccer, the World Tennis Association, the PGA, the LPGA, IndyCar, NASCAR, and the NCAA postponed or canceled almost every single athletic event that was scheduled to air on live television that spring and summer.

For sports fans, this was devastating. For television networks like ESPN, which rely on live sporting events to fill their broadcast schedules, this was a *very* big problem.

The ESPN (which is owned by Disney) business model is to spend billions of dollars on the rights to air live sports, then pack a bunch of other talking heads programs, pre- and post-game shows, and *SportsCenter* constantly playing on a loop when they have nothing else to air. Without any games being played, there were big gaps in the broadcast schedule, and not that much to talk about on the periphery shows, which would normally be dissecting what happened in the games.

ESPN's producers tried to steer the programming to stories about how the coronavirus was impacting sports, but the public's interest in that seemed so minuscule compared to how the virus was affecting everything else in the world.

They could break down the NFL free agency—the NFL is always a hot topic. But the NFL season seemed so far off, in that spring especially. They tried to obtain rights to replay classic NBA and MLB games, to little avail. Their viewership numbers in March were nearly 50% lower than the previous year, which is an insane drop by any measure.

The only option they had for original entertainment was ESPN8: The Ocho. They aired blocks and blocks of novelty "athletic" competitions. Viewers could tune into such events as cherry pit spitting, arm wrestling, sign spinning, stone skipping, slippery stair racing, and many other wacky events. One of the favorites was marble runs, where insanely intricate courses and events were constructed and then a "team" of marbles would compete for superiority.

Plenty of families who were starving for any sort of athletic endeavors on television watched when they needed a little break from the pandemic news.

As far as ESPN viewership went, they completed production on *The Last Dance*, the 10-part documentary about Michael Jordan and the Chicago Bulls dynasty from the 1990's. They moved the series premier from June to April, to stop the ratings from hemorrhaging. It worked. The show averaged 5.6 million viewers during the 10-episode run, and it became a pop culture phenomenon.

Education

Swings Were Removed from Playgrounds

The swing is the ultimate piece of playground equipment. Simply two metal chains connected to some reinforced rubber, but when hung from a metal bar, it gives those who have mastered the leg pump the ability to fly over and over (and over) again. And for little kids with a parent pushing them, it allows them to dabble with the feeling of being out of control, but returning to the comfort of their parent's hands on the way back down. No physical exertion and blisters like the monkey bars, no rough rides like the spiral slide, and no nausea-inducing spinning like the merry-go-round. The swing is the place one can go by themselves and transport to a different world.

Or it used to be.

As the pandemic swept through the nation, schools were forced to make many difficult decisions to keep their students and staff safe, and this was one of the more preposterous ones: the swings had to come down.

The main concern was transmission of the virus through touching shared surfaces. Swings, with their chains and seats frequently touched by multiple children, were seen as high-risk areas for the spread of COVID-19. To minimize the risk of transmission, and to make more room on the playground for students to socially distance, many schools chose to remove the swings entirely.

As we found out eventually, the virus didn't really spread through surface contact. At the time, that science wasn't completely understood. However, the schools decided to play it safe and remove one of the main sources of joy from the playground. It was hard to blame them in the moment, but easy to criticize it now.

For many children, the return of the swings was a momentous occasion, a sign that things were slowly starting to return to normal. And as they swung back and forth, feeling the wind rushing through their hair, it was a reminder of their resilience and adaptability of kids.

Students Were Required to Wear Masks All Day at School

Masks are the absolute worst. Nobody likes wearing them. They are hot, and when you breathe, the condensation from your breath adds moisture to your lips and cheeks and chin. Even the best cloth masks rub on the bridge of your nose and back of your ears. The mask's biggest feature is their biggest weakness. They prevent your breath from properly escaping and instead circulate it right back to your nose. The freshest smelling mouth is gross in a mask.

Many fully grown adults got through the pandemic but were barely able to tolerate the masks in short bursts, such as going into a grocery store or in a doctor's office. But what we asked our kids to do—wear a face mask for the entire day, from morning bus stop pickup to afternoon bus stop drop off—was kind of a low-key torture that was one of the worst parts of the pandemic. This might have been a case of the cure being worse than the disease.

As school districts across the country made the decision to require masks to keep their students and staff safe from the virus, some parents and teachers expressed worries that the use of masks had negative side effects on children. Some students had difficulty breathing. Younger kids had their language development hindered, unable to see a speaker's mouth move combined with the muffling effect of a mask. Others reported concerns of stunted social and emotional growth, leading to feelings of anxiety.

One of the more confounding realities of the pandemic was that children were not nearly as susceptible to the virus as other age groups. Children ages 17 and under made up less than 10 percent of all cases in the United States and accounted for only .13% of the deaths. However, they were inordinately affected the most, forced to wear a mask for at least seven hours a day with very few breaks. It seemed like a bad concept to some, except the policymakers.

The argument was that even if the kids weren't likely to get seriously sick themselves, they could still transmit the disease to someone else back at their home. For many, that argument really didn't hold water, and certainly didn't justify the irreparable damage that masks caused to our children. We definitely know it affected them, but we may not completely realize the full effect it had for some time.

Schools Introduced Distance Learning With Zoom Calls

In March 2020, most public elementary schools essentially shut down in-person learning for the remainder of the 2020 school year. They had good intentions. Some schools started out closing for just 2 weeks, which turned into two more weeks, and then that slid into just shutting it down for the rest of the year to get to the summer.

Some districts were caught flat footed without a real plan. To be fair, the situation and the outlook could change almost every single day, and the science behind the virus (mask efficacy, transmission risk, etc.) was very fluid. No one saw a global event at the magnitude of COVID-19 coming, so being a little unprepared at the beginning could be forgiven.

As parents, we showed grace, and gave the school districts the summer to prepare a plan for the 2020-2021 school year that could keep everyone safe, but most importantly get the kids learning again.

More than three-quarters of the 50 largest school districts in the United States decided to start the school year remotely, and most other smaller districts followed.

The concept of having elementary-aged kids sitting at home, receiving an hour or two of remote lessons, then being left on their own to complete assignments, and to pass this off as "education" is one of the most flawed ideas that came from COVID-19. Plain and simple, it did not work.

For teachers, the task was impossible. Elementary students are difficult to keep engaged even in the best of times. While their classroom was a living room or a bedroom with all the stimuli (devices, video games, Netflix), was a ridiculous challenge. If you were lucky enough to monitor a teaching session, half of the Zoom call was teachers telling students to mute themselves, reminding them not to have their pets on camera, and please no doodling on the screen. The portion of the day where students were left on their own was no better on the kids. They would have no help if the assignments were confusing or they had technology problems. Their teachers were busy with something else, and their two working parents were, you know, working.

If we can commit to one thing moving forward, let's commit to ditching distance learning forever and burying those stupid iPads in the same field they dumped all those unsold E.T. games for Atari (ask Siri).

Schools Turned Off
Their Water Fountains

A small and slightly trivial change that many students and teachers noticed when they returned to school after the COVID-19 pandemic hit was that the water fountains were turned off.

One of the main reasons for the shutdown of water fountains was the concern about the transmission of the virus through touching shared surfaces. Water fountains, with their buttons and spouts that are frequently touched by multiple people, were seen as high-risk areas for the spread of COVID-19. To minimize the risk of transmission, schools chose to turn off the water fountains entirely.

Water fountains can be difficult to clean and disinfect, especially during a pandemic.

While the shutdown of water fountains may have been deemed necessary for the safety of students and staff, it was a creature comfort many missed. Water fountains were a source of refreshment and convenience. There is nothing better than drinking right from a water fountain, especially right after gym class, or fresh from the school yard during recess on a hot day. A whole generation may never know about counting to five while the person ahead of you takes their drink. We always had that limit, and if you wanted another drink, back to the end of the line you went. No hogging. And no drinking all the water in the Mississippi River.

Despite the weirdness of seeing the water fountains with safety tape over them, many schools were able to find creative solutions to keep their students hydrated. Water bottle filling stations were installed in many schools, providing students with a convenient way to refill their bottles and stay hydrated throughout the day. They are operated via touchless sensors, so there were less transmission risks.

If you haven't been to a school recently, it's bizarre. Every single student has their own reusable water bottle. Every. Single. Student. What did previous generations do when we didn't always have non-stop access to our own water supply? We didn't dry up and disintegrate to dust. We were just fine. Big Water Bottle has this generation wrapped around their finger. I am looking directly at you, Hydro Flask.

Students Had to Eat Lunch at Their Desks

One of the biggest changes for students when they returned to school after the pandemic were the protocols put in place to help maintain social distancing. The biggest disruptor was skipping the lunchroom and instead grabbing school lunch and eating it alone at their own desk. Gone were the days of crowded cafeteria tables and socializing over lunch, replaced instead with a new and unfamiliar routine known as "desk dining."

For many students, the idea of eating at their desks was a ridiculous and unnecessary change. After all, the cafeteria was a beloved part of the school experience, a place to socialize and relax with friends over a shared meal. And with so many other measures in place to keep students safe, such as masks and social distancing, it seemed unnecessary and even a bit foolish to eliminate this beloved part of the school day.

Kids are in school to learn and be educated, no doubt. But one of the most important things kids learn in school is how to be social human beings. The lunch table can be the wild west, but it's where kids learn how to be good people.

Restaurants had effectively removed the mask protocol for indoor dining. Patrons had to wear their masks to their seats, but once there, they could take the mask off for the entirety of the meal. It seemed like kids could handle this same type of rule in the lunchroom.

While the switch to desk dining may have been well-intentioned, it was not without its challenges. For many students, the loss of the social aspect of the cafeteria was taking away one of their favorite parts of the day. The chance to socialize and talk about anything but class. Some students reported feeling isolated and lonely while eating at their desks, with no one to talk to or share their meals with.

But despite the protests and complaints of students, schools across the country made the decision to switch to desk dining to keep their students and staff safe during the pandemic. The reasoning behind the change was that it would reduce the risk of transmission by eliminating crowded cafeteria spaces and shared surfaces.

School Field Trips Were
Canceled

It was a decision that disappointed and frustrated many students and teachers alike: the cancellation of field trips due to the COVID-19 pandemic. Field trips are the most beloved part of the school experience, a chance to learn and explore beyond the classroom walls. A day to be around your classmates, but in a whole new environment, like the zoo, or a Science Museum is the reward for getting through the mundane and monotonous.

But as the pandemic swept through the nation, schools were forced to make difficult decisions to keep their students and staff safe. To some, the cancellation of field trips seemed like an unnecessary and even foolish decision. Students were already wearing masks, already getting on a school bus, already near other students and their teachers. The only additional variable going on a field trip introduced was a new location to explore. With the added benefits of experiential learning and cultural enrichment, it seemed like a shame to miss out on such an important part of the school experience.

Despite the protests and complaints of students, some parents, and even some teachers, schools across the country made the decision to cancel field trips to keep their communities safe. The reasoning behind the decision was that field trips often involved close contact with large groups of people and could be difficult to monitor and control in terms of social distancing and hygiene. By canceling field trips, schools were able to reduce the risk of transmission and keep their students and staff safe, or at least say they checked that box.

A lot of "leadership" in the pandemic was just saying "No", generally erring on the side of caution. Nobody wanted to be the principal who made the news because he okayed the field trip to the zoo where the whole second grade got the coronavirus. Due to their caution, many kids were deprived of the age-old tradition of the field trip.

Close Contacts Triggered Mandatory Quarantines

With school back open, there were dozens of safety procedures in place to prevent the spread of COVID-19 between those in the school. Face coverings were required for everyone in school buildings, classrooms were set up to maintain social distancing of 6 feet, and student groups limited the number of students who could be exposed to a positive case.

When a family notified the school nurse that their child had tested positive for COVID-19, the school worked with health officials from the State Department of Health and the county Public Health Department to do contact tracing to identify the close contacts they needed to notify. Close contacts were defined as anyone who was within 6 feet of the ill person for more than 15 minutes, even if both individuals were wearing face coverings. The bottom line was that if the person next to your student tested positive for coronavirus, you would get one of these emails:

Hello Parents,

Your child has been identified as a close contact of someone who has tested positive for Covid. Your child last had contact on November 16, and we require a 10-day quarantine.

As a close contact, your child should stay home and not take part in any activities/sports for 10 days, which is through November 26. Your child can return to school on Monday, November 30, so long as they do not develop symptoms or test positive during this time.

Take care,
School Nurse

It was a frustrating policy for many students. Because a single student had a positive test, any other student near them in class, a whole classroom, or even the entire school could be shut down, depending on contact. If the masks that the kids were required to wear all day worked, wouldn't that prevent transmission? Instead, it was yet another disruption to the learning for the students, and another example of how the play-it-safe policymakers hurt the students.

Senior Prom and Graduation Were Canceled

Two of the biggest rites of passage for high school kids are the senior prom and graduation. In the spring of 2020, one of the harderst decisions for school districts across the country was to cancel both events.

For some students, the cancellation of prom and graduation seemed like an unnecessary, cruel punishment, and a missed opportunity to celebrate everyone's hard work and accomplishments. Students had been remote learning for the better part of the spring, and having an opportunity to celebrate would have meant a lot. But both events attract huge crowds, and that was a problem for policy makers.

Many seniors will forever be considered the Forgotten Class—those who didn't get to celebrate the two biggest moments in their high school years. It was one of the most heartbreaking things that happened to our kids, another way that the pandemic ripped apart our youths' social lives.

One of the bright sides of COVID-19 was the YouTube show that actor John Krasinski created, called Some Good News (SGN). It focused on highlighting good news at the time, with a bunch of cameos from big name celebrities, such as Brad Pitt, Ryan Reynolds, and Martha Stewart. On April 17, Krasinski hosted a livestream virtual prom for all the kids who wouldn't be able to attend their own proms. He had artists such as Billie Eilish and the Jonas Brothers play some of their music and had a live DJ playing music for the kids to enjoy, just like a regular prom.

A few days later, he did a graduation show for the kids who wouldn't have otherwise had any ceremony to attend. Krasinski invited new graduates onto the show, who got to ask questions of his celebrity guests--Oprah Winfrey, Jon Stewart, and Steven Spielberg. Talk about some great commencement speakers!

Was it the same as the real thing? No, it wasn't. But they both were very touching and memorable videos that helped make the days of millions of people a little brighter. The show's slogan was "No matter how bad it gets, there is still some good in the world", and it was an extremely well-done show amid a very weird time.

College Students Attended
All Virtual Classes

For the Forgotten Class of seniors who graduated ceremony-less in the spring of 2020, those students who went on to college in the fall of 2020 kept the weirdness right on rolling. They were the class of students that got to start college during a pandemic, with all their classes being attended virtually.

Normally, the freshmen year at college is a year for wing-spreading: moving away from parents for the first time; meeting a whole new group of friends that aren't from the same hometown; and independently navigating a college campus while pursuing higher education.

During the pandemic, however, nothing was normal. Freshman year of college was significantly altered. Some colleges didn't even open student housing for incoming freshmen. For those who did, the dormitories had a ton of restrictions, sometimes forbidding students to visit other floors. Cafeterias were replaced with grab-and-go meals. Weekly COVID-19 tests were the norm in some schools. Dormitory rooms felt a little like prison cells, and the students were serving sentences isolated from loved ones.

Most colleges were virtual learning only. Students would listen to lectures and take notes from their dorm rooms, rather than 500-seat lecture halls. Zoom socials and virtual study groups were the full extent of the socialization many students experienced. Additionally, athletic events, one of the hallmarks of the college life, were played without fans in attendance.

Some students saw this huge shift coming and opted to take a gap year, typically taken by high school graduates prior to starting college, when universities switched to remote learning. Many factors, including financial difficulties, the diminished college experience due to online learning, and pandemic-related stress contributed to the trend of taking a gap year a more popular route. In fact, incoming freshmen enrollment fell by 13.1% in fall 2020.

The college experience has always been more than just getting an advanced education, and with the fun and exciting parts of college removed from the equation, what was left was kind of terrible way to start the journey of higher learning.

Private Schools Stayed Open
While Public Schools Closed

COVID-19 exposed a variety of ironies and inequalities in society. One of the most striking examples of this was how private and public schools reacted differently during the early months of the crisis.

While public schools were forced by the government to shut their doors and pivot to remote learning, many private schools remained open.

At first glance, this might not seem particularly ironic. After all, private schools are typically known for their smaller class sizes, more resources, and more flexible schedules. These factors could have made it easier for them to implement social distancing measures and keep students safe. Many private schools had the financial resources to invest in additional safety measures to help with cleaning and disinfection. Public schools, on the other hand, often struggled to afford these same resources, even as they were being mandated to implement them.

Private schools, by their very nature, are designed to cater to the needs of a select group of students. They often have more stringent admissions criteria, and they charge tuition fees. This means that they are typically attended by students from more privileged backgrounds, who are less likely to be impacted by the virus in the first place.

Public schools, on the other hand, serve a more diverse population of students. Kids living in higher levels of poverty were more likely to attend public school and have more difficulty with distance learning. U.S. counties with the lowest median income had death rates at least two times higher than that of the counties with the highest income.

The irony, then, is that the schools that were most able to remain open during the pandemic were the ones that were serving the students who were least likely to be impacted by it. Meanwhile, the schools that were serving the most vulnerable students were the ones that were forced to close their doors.

It was one of the many ways that more affluent people were less affected by COVID-19 and another example of how policymakers may have inadvertently hurt the students they were trying to protect.

Students Switched Over to A/B Class Schedules

After the pandemic shut the 2019-2020 school year down, school leaders and parents were faced with a challenging decision about whether to continue with distance learning or attempt a more complex approach known as a "hybrid" model starting in the Fall of 2020.

This approach involved a combination of in-person classes, online instruction, and a lengthy set of regulations designed to limit the spread of COVID-19. The hybrid model aimed to meet students' academic, emotional, and social needs by bringing them back together with teachers and peers, which was seen as both important and urgent after months of isolation and online lessons.

However, reopening schools under strict capacity limits and social distancing requirements meant that many students had to attend classes on rotating schedules: A/B Scheduling.

Monday and Tuesday, Group A would attend in-person classes while Group B participated in virtual learning. On Thursday and Friday, the groups would switch, with Group A participating in virtual learning and Group B attending in-person classes. On Wednesday, everybody stayed home so they could clean the school. By staggering the schedules and reducing the number of students in the building at any given time, schools were able to reduce the risk of transmission and create a safer learning environment.

This raised concerns for teachers, who had to manage split classrooms, and parents who had to manage their children's weird schedules, as they still only attended school twice a week, and may have siblings with different schedules in the same household. In essence, it was a challenging logistical issue that caused significant concern for everyone who was involved.

A lot of people just wanted the schools re-opened completely, but reluctantly accepted hybrid as the next best option to get students back in the classroom. The results of the experiment went about how you could imagine.

In general, the experience of being in the classroom was great. Less students, less distraction, and more of the teachers undivided attention for each student. It mimicked more of a private school environment, with smaller class size and devoted attention from the teacher. It made you think about what the ideal class size and the ideal structure would be. Half of a classroom full of kids worked very well.

Conversely, the experience of learnings on their home days felt like not really going to school at all. The teacher had very little time to help the students, apart from a short overview at the beginning of the day. It was up to the students and their parents to figure out what work was assigned and to plow through the mounds of stapled workbook packets and iPads with bundles of learning apps.

The software loaded on the iPads ranged from barely usable to sometimes horrendously bad. Terrible user interfaces and difficult tools to take screenshots and submit work were the standard. Specifically, two popular learning platforms, Seesaw and IXL, notoriously created more problems than the actual curriculum. Teachers would be frustrated because half of their job was technical service support. Students were so frustrated with the technology that they would just shut down. All in all, it was not the ideal learning environment.

Understandably, some parents just developed the "To hell with this!" attitude and let their kids off the hook when it came time to turn in daily assignments. In return, teachers and administrators stopped marking work late and many districts refused to give students failing grades.

Most kids got the best learning environment for the two days in the classroom, and then got the feeling of being left behind on the two days distance learning from home. It was a weird way to try balance the classroom and a poor way to sustain learning momentum with students throughout the week.

But what about Wednesdays? That is the part that is most interesting. Why did the the school need to have Wednesdays off? Was it that the classrooms got so epically destroyed on Monday and Tuesday that it was forced to take a full day to put it back together for the other group of students to use on Thursday and Friday? It shouldn't have, with only half the school being there you would think half the mess.

Was it that the school was being overrun with germs? Students and teachers were required to wear a face mask the entire day. Coronavirus spread mainly through airborne particles and droplets. There shouldn't have been that many particles in the air if everyone was masked up. A proper spraying down of each desktop or workspace should have been an adequate precaution if one was worried about the virus living on surfaces for extended periods of time. Wiping down each desktop shouldn't take all day, should it?

Why did the schools push for that middle day to be an everyone-stays-home day? One answer was the teachers' unions. There was a study that found that school districts with lengthier collective bargaining agreements were less likely to start fall 2020 with full in-person instruction, spend more time in distance learning, and were less likely to ever have in-person classes at all in the fall semester.

Teachers' unions are some one of the most powerful organizations in the country. While the decision to shut schools down in the spring of 2020 was largely decided at each state level, by the fall of 2020, most of the 13,000 school districts were left on their own to make their reopening plans. At the local level, teachers' unions are even stronger. Many of the smaller school districts waited for larger neighboring districts to put a policy in place, and then just let the policy cascade to them. The mighty teachers' union was responsible for setting the guidelines for re-opening.

Teachers' unions utilize master negotiators to define their collective bargaining agreements. Every bone of contention is looked at as an opportunity to claw something back in their next contract. For instance, the teachers' union might say that they don't want the schools open at all—it's much too dangerous for their teachers to be teaching under the circumstances. But they may be willing to compromise, perhaps, with a hybrid arrangement, if it meant maybe a 5% salary raise, guaranteed smaller class sizes, or better health care benefits during the next contract negotiations. Typically, there is never a concession without a return.

It was reasonable to anticipate that the teachers' unions would impede decisions to reopen schools, just as we would anticipate their efforts to push for more education funding in the state, smaller class sizes, and better sick leave for teachers. The union's duty is to safeguard and speak for the interests of teachers, and their effectiveness is measured by how well they fulfill this responsibility.

At the end of the day, the decision to shut down schools and then reopen them with hybrid learning plans boiled down to two questions. People decided how to judge that decision based on their responses.

How much risk do you think in-person teaching caused the students and teachers?

How much damage did distance learning cause the children in development, both educationally and socially?

If you thought the risk of the virus was higher than the damage done by distance learning, you most likely didn't have any hard feelings towards the teachers' union. If you thought that the risk of the pandemic was minuscule because children weren't really affected by the virus like adults, but that the damage that children suffered from a year of distance learning may be irreparable, then at least a portion of your displeasure could be directed at the teachers' union.

Shopping

Grocery Stores Added Arrow Stickers to Control Aisle Flow

The pandemic brought about a host of changes to the way we live our daily lives, and one of the most visible of these was the way that stores laid out their physical space and managed their people flow. To promote social distancing and reduce the spread of the virus, many stores converted all their aisles to one-way only, with arrows directing the flow of traffic.

In all honesty, it was probably one of the better ideas that came out of the pandemic. What it made shoppers do was think about what they were doing in the store, rather than floating endlessly without a purpose. Pre-pandemic, a shopper could show up to the supermarket with a few ideas of what they wanted, and just kind of wing it. But during the pandemic, everybody had to step up their shopping game.

Shoppers would get their carts and set off on their journey. They would start in the produce section, move past the deli and meat departments, then hit all the canned, bottled, boxed, and bagged sections in the middle of the store, on their way back to the dairy section. Everyone was focused, alert, and hyper-aware of others.

Before checkout, they would swing through the home goods section for another couple bottles of Lysol and a quick check to see if they had any toilet paper in stock (spoiler alert: they did not). All the while, arrows guided them up and down each aisle.

The goal was to maintain their distance from the shopper ahead and behind them, equidistantly. There wasn't a lot of time to meander, nobody wanted lollygaggers. Why are you taking that long to look at the ingredients in Prego spaghetti sauce? It's a pandemic—just throw it in the cart and keep on moving!

If a shopper needed time to shop, that's what InstaCart was there for. But if a shopper was headed into a store, they needed to have a list, sorted by department, and stick to it. And heaven forbid, the last anyone wanted was to forget something on their list. It meant they would basically have to start the whole process over, headed back to the beginning of the journey by the produce section, and try to remember what they missed on the next trip through the store.

Shoppers Wore Protective Gloves in Grocery Stores

One trend that was popular during the pandemic's beginning was people wearing gloves while shopping at grocery stores. Whether shopping, running errands, or simply going for a walk, there was a subset of the population who turned to donning a pair of gloves to achieve an extra barrier of protection from the virus. Whether this actually provided the extra protection can be left up for debate.

Although wearing medical gloves, which are typically made of natural latex or other stretchy synthetic materials, during essential errands may appear to offer protection against COVID-19, it's not entirely accurate. Gloves can be misleading. People might assume that they are safeguarded and then use gloves to touch their face or themselves. Once the gloves are contaminated, they are as ineffective as using bare hands. This can create a false sense of security, leading to less cautious hand hygiene practices like avoiding face touching or handwashing.

Cross-contamination frequently occurred while putting on and taking off gloves. Like wearing masks or cloth face coverings, wearing gloves necessitated a specific technique, and some people just didn't follow the proper way to use them effectively.

Not everyone should have been wearing the gloves at all. According to the CDC, people who are caring for someone who is infected with COVID-19 should wear disposable gloves when cleaning surfaces, washing dishes, and doing laundry for a sick person, but not necessarily those who are squeezing avocados in the grocery store.

The CDC also warned that the public over buying and using gloves for mundane tasks was going to cause a shortage of gloves for medical staffs that needed them more.

The biggest thing that gloves did was identify the people who were the most cautious and maybe a little paranoid about catching the virus. You could spot these extra-cautious people by their double masks, gloves, and other extra precautions they took in public places.

Shoppers Wiped Down
Groceries When They Got Them
Home

For some people got their groceries home from the store, the battle was just beginning. There was a huge trend in the beginning months of the pandemic where people would let their groceries sit on the counter (or outside on the porch for deliveries). They would also wipe down the groceries individually with disinfectant spray or wipes.

To be fair to everybody, at the very beginning, there was a tremendous number of theories and much speculation about how the disease was spreading and what could be done to slow down the transmission.

In late March, the worry about the transmission of the virus through surfaces arose following research published in the esteemed New England Journal of Medicine. The study indicated that the coronavirus could possibly survive on cardboard for a maximum of 24 hours and on metal and plastic for two to three days, but only in a laboratory-controlled environment. However, this research did not consider external factors such as sunlight or temperatures outside the lab setting that could potentially inactivate the virus. Moreover, the study did not factor in the minimum amount of the virus required to transmit it to another person, solely stating the virus's ability to survive.

However, the damage had already been done, and people were paranoid about bringing items into their home that could potentially get their family sick.

It reached such a wide fervor that the FDA felt compelled to chime in and tweeted the following on April 16, 2020:

> FDA has heard your concerns about shopping for #food safely. We want to assure you there is currently NO evidence of human or animal food or food packaging being associated with transmission of the #COVID19.

This confirmed to a lot of people that it might be time to reconsider the practice, especially if the extra effort was causing stress, as there was no real risk of getting COVID-19 from the groceries.

Stores Required Customers Give Each Other Space in Checkout Line

Another great protocol that was implemented during the pandemic that was the six-foot rule in the checkout lanes. It made people show a little respect for the other people in the line as they waited.

Prior to the pandemic, there were some people who had absolutely no concept of other people's personal space. When someone checks out, they unload the 50+ items from their cart onto the conveyor belt. The ones who are ultra-conscience will then take one of those little plastic dividers and place it down behind their items. This is meant as a marker to separate items for the cashier, who isn't paying close attention to which customer is trying to buy the Oreos.

It was NEVER meant as an open invitation to the next customer behind them in line to come up within six inches and start unloading their items up on the belt as well. These people act like if they can just get their items on the belt, it will somehow make the whole process go faster. Here is a very special note to that specific customer:

> Hey lady, I sure hope you found all your items ok. Listen, the cashier can only scan items so fast, and she is busting her butt. You are three back in line. Just chill out, you will get your turn. The aisle sign is still illuminated—she's not going on break. The person ahead of you does not want your breathing down their neck. Are you feeling anxious? Relax. Just turn your head, there is so much to see while you wait. Why does M&Ms make so many varieties, like Nut Brownie? Who is asking for that flavor? Yuck. What the hell did Prince Harry get himself into with this Meghan Markle psycho? Yeeesh. Is the line between breath mint and candy becoming dangerously blurred with all these fruity flavors? Hmmm...

The six-foot rule put an end to this behavior. Walmart, Target, and Kohl's and many others started asking customers to give each other six feet in the checkout lanes. They even put stickers down on the floor to show people exactly where six feet was, because God knows people are not good at math or judging distance. The markers were a way to keep their customers comfortable. Many are still on the floors today and here's hoping that they stick around forever.

Stores Installed Plexiglass Barriers for Their Cashiers

From the other side of the conveyor belt, the grocery store cashier got a raw deal during the pandemic. They were considered essential workers during the COVID-19 pandemic and continued to work to ensure that people had access to essential items such as food and household supplies. Cashiers had to adapt to new safety measures such as wearing masks and gloves, frequently washing their hands, and sanitizing their workstations regularly.

One of the very first things that popped up immediately in any place of business with direct interaction with customers was plexiglass screens. Banks, gas stations, liquor stores, smoke shops, groceries stores, and pharmacies all seemingly installed them overnight. It wasn't quite clear where all this plexiglass came from, or if there were companies doing all these retrofits in businesses so quickly. If so, they must have made a ton of money, because one day no businesses had them, and the next day, they were ubiquitous.

The barriers also raised a host of logistical issues. Many workers found that they had to shout or use hand gestures to be heard or understood through the mask and plexiglass, plus the noise of the store. Constantly repeating things was inconvenient and tiring. Customers, on the other hand, often had difficulty hearing or seeing what they were being told, which led to misunderstandings and frustration. People took for granted how much seeing someone's facial gestures as they spoke helped them understand what they were saying.

Cashiers also had to deal with increased demand and long lines as people stocked up on supplies. In turn, this led to higher stress levels and longer working hours. Many grocery stores also had to adjust their hours and services, such as offering online ordering and curbside pickup, to meet the needs of customers while adhering to safety guidelines.

Overall, working as a grocery store cashier during the COVID-19 pandemic was challenging, but it was also an essential service that provided a sense of purpose and pride for those who continued to work on the front lines. Society was very grateful for these workers.

Customers Went Overboard Wiping Down the Credit Card Readers

This was a sign written on piece of paper, taped to the bottom of credit card reader, at a popular local grocery store:

> Attention Customers:
>
> Please stop spraying our credit card readers with disinfectant spray. Several machines have had to be replaced. Your safety is our priority--we clean all of our machines regularly.
>
> Thanks,
> Management

During the beginning of the pandemic, there was a widespread belief that the virus could survive on surfaces for extended periods of time, including credit card readers. As a result, people started excessively spraying down credit card readers with disinfectants or cleaning agents, thinking this act would prevent them from catching the virus.

However, it was later found that the risk of transmission through surfaces is quite low, if not altogether impossible. This was especially true if people practiced good hygiene by washing their hands regularly and avoiding touching their face. The primary mode of transmission for COVID-19 was through respiratory droplets that was released when an infected person talked, coughed, or sneezed.

Still, this did not stop the emboldened few from setting their own sanitization protocols for the store or the gas pump keypads. Shoppers could be seen wiping down credit card readers with Lysol wipes, spraying them with bottles of disinfectants, and even pouring hand sanitizer directly onto the keypad.

Excessive cleaning of credit card readers damaged the machines and made them less effective or even unusable. Plus, these people were overlooking the most easy and controllable sanitization, which they could do on their own: wash your hands. It was the one thing experts said repeatedly from the beginning, and the best strategy for staying safe.

Customer Waited in Line While Stores Limited Shoppers in Store

In the first week of April 2020, big retailers started to enforce customer limits to promote social distancing and reduce the spread of the virus, and to do everything they could to remain open.

Walmart and Target declared their intention to restrict the number of people allowed inside their stores at any given time as a measure to encourage social distancing. Both stores said they would meter the amount of guests inside and keep the capacity down to roughly 20 percent of each store's capacity.

At each store, it was an employee's job to stand outside the door with a clicker, and as one person left, another person could be admitted inside. The lines of people would spread out six feet apart along the building, and grow quite long during busy shopping times as people waited their turn to shop.

The virus was thought to spread more easily in crowded spaces, and limiting the number of people present at any given time would theoretically reduce the risk of transmission, while allowing the stores to stay open. The stores were looking out for their customers and their employees, but also the bottom line.

These policies trickled down to other stores that were allowed to remain operational. Some stores struggled to balance the need for social distancing with the need to keep their doors open and serve their customers. They had to find ways to manage lines and reduce the amount of time that people spent inside the store, which was not always easy.

At the same time, the customer limits also became a source of irritation and frustration for some people. They were a reminder of the barriers that had been put in place to keep us safe, and the ways in which we were all struggling to navigate this new normal. Some people found it inconvenient or annoying to have to wait in line or limit the amount of time they spent shopping, while others saw it as a sign of unnecessary paranoia or overreaction.

Stores Limited the Amount of Fresh Water Each Customer Could Buy

As the COVID-19 pandemic swept through the country, people began to stockpile supplies in case of a long-term lockdown. Just like when bad weather is forecasted, it triggered hoarding for the people of the United States. And one item that seemed to be at the top of everyone's list was water.

During the beginning of the frenzied water buying, people rushed to stock up before the supplies ran out. It was not uncommon to see people pushing shopping carts filled to the brim with cases of bottled water or filling up jugs and containers at the store's water stations. While it didn't get the same amount of publicity as toilet paper did, it drew attention.

But why all the fuss over H2O? To understand this phenomenon, we must first look at the psychology of panic buying. When faced with a crisis, our brains tend to go into survival mode. We become more risk-averse and prioritize the acquisition of resources that we believe will help us weather the storm. For some, this meant stockpiling water.

Some people feared that if their state was ordered into a lockdown, they would be cut off from basic supplies. Water is a particularly important resource, as it is essential for human survival. Without it, we would quickly become dehydrated and suffer from a host of health problems. It's no wonder that people were eager to stock up on as much water as they could get their hands on.

After the initial wave and complaints from other shoppers, many stores stepped in and imposed limits on how much water each person could buy. It seemed that no matter where you went, there were signs reading "2 gallons per customer" or "limit of 4 bottles per purchase." This was a good step by the stores to place the priority people over profits in these situations.

The only logical flaw in all this panic buying was that most of the United States' drinking water is very good, and nearly endless. There also wasn't a single instance of COVID-19 attributed to water-based transmission. The decision to stockpile water didn't come from a sound position, but rather from some human instinct to hoard supplies during times of uncertainty.

Ma an Pa Stores Were
Closed Down While
Big Box Stores Stayed Open

It was a confusing time for small business owners as the COVID-19 pandemic swept through the United States. On the one hand, they were being told to shut down to slow the spread of the virus. On the other hand, big box stores were allowed to remain open, seemingly without consequence.

This double standard was met with frustration from small business owners, who saw it as a blatant example of hypocrisy. They were being told to sacrifice their livelihoods for the greater good, while the big corporations were allowed to continue raking in profits.

Why were big box stores able to stay open while the small businesses were forced to close? To understand this paradox, we must examine the role that these stores play in our economy and society.

Big box stores like Walmart and Target were considered essential businesses, meaning that they provide goods and services that are necessary for the daily functioning of our society. These stores are often the only source of groceries and other household items in rural or low-income areas, and they serve as a lifeline for many people who rely on them for necessities.

But for many small business owners, the decision to keep the big box stores open while forcing them to close was a bitter pill to swallow. These businesses, which often had limited resources and thin profit margins to begin with, were now being hit hard by the pandemic. Many were forced to lay off employees or close their doors for good.

The hypocrisy of this situation was not lost on the public, who took to social media in an effort to to express their outrage. The hashtag #smallbusinessmatters trended, as people called on the government to provide financial assistance for these struggling businesses.

And indeed, the government did eventually step in with programs like the Paycheck Protection Program (PPP) and the Economic Injury Disaster Loan (EIDL) program. These initiatives provided much-needed financial relief to small businesses, helping them to weather the storm of the pandemic. However, for many small businesses, the damage had already been done.

Fitting Rooms Were Closed Down

Many stores adopted the policy of closing their fitting rooms as a safety protocol. The idea was that fitting rooms were small by nature. As a customer tried on clothes, respiratory droplets could be spread if the customer talked, coughed, or sneezed. The next customer could pick up the virus from a shared surface or even if they were in the next fitting room. Also, there would be a theoretical risk of transmission to another customers or employee who later picked up the same items. Therefore, the fitting rooms were shut down.

For many shoppers, this was a major inconvenience. After all, trying on clothes is an integral part of the shopping experience. You must see if the look is right in those special flattering mirrors retailers use.

But with the closure of fitting rooms, shoppers were left to rely on their own judgment, the help of a salesperson, or encouraged to buy a couple different sizes and return the ones that didn't fit. Predictably, this led to an increase in returns and exchanges, as people found that the clothes they had purchased didn't fit as expected. This meant an extra trip to the store and contact with an employee who would be processing the return.

Why were the fitting rooms deemed such a risk? There wasn't a single case of COVID-19 that was linked to trying on clothing. Could there be an ulterior motive? With a lot of the Covid protocols, there seemed to be.

The shutdown of the fitting room came at the same time as shopper restrictions. Perhaps stores didn't want people spending time trying on clothes while people were literally lining up outside to come in and buy things.

It may have been another one of the ways that the pandemic was a blessing in disguise for retailers. Some stores have always hated the idea of dressing rooms, and the pandemic was a great cover to close them indefinitely. Loss prevention was greatly helped by not having dressing rooms, as people couldn't use the one area in the store without cameras as a place to conceal items. Believe it or not, some people are animals, and extremely gross things are done in dressing rooms that need to be cleaned. Many retail workers were happy not to deal with the headache of the fitting room mess.

Stores Created Time Slots for the Immunocompromised to Shop

One measure that was put in place at many stores was the creation of special shopping times for the elderly and immunocompromised. These special shopping times were designed to allow people who were at higher risk for severe illness from COVID-19 to shop in a safer environment. By limiting the number of people in the store and providing a dedicated time for these individuals to shop, stores were able to create a safer shopping experience.

Elderly people and those with compromised immune systems were at significantly higher risk for COVID-19. They were significantly more likely to experience complications from the virus and have a much higher mortality rate. Basically, the entire pandemic response—masks, social distancing, quarantines—were all done to keep the elderly and immunocompromised safe.

At some point, there should be a study done to see if this was the best response. Some could argue we shouldn't have shut down any businesses or any parts of society, and instead protected the elderly and immunocompromised using a different strategy, but that debate is for a different time.

Target, Whole Foods, Aldi, and Dollar General were examples of stores who adopted a policy where at least one day a week there was an hour dedicated to people of a certain age. Most other regional or local stores followed suit with their own similar policies, as the goal was to keep their customers safe, but also to follow the industry leader's examples. As with a lot of the policies set during the pandemic, the leaders in each area would act first and figure out the strategy, and then everyone beneath them would just let the protocols cascade down to them.

The special shopping times were met with mostly positive reactions from the public. In some cases, younger shoppers had to wait outside for the time slot to pass, but it was a minor annoyance. The time slots were almost always the first hour of the day that the store was open, while most people were still asleep. The elderly got their shopping out of the way in an empty store, without any of those pesky whippersnappers to get in their way. This was probably the way they would have wanted it to be all along.

Corona Beer Sales Plummeted

It was a strange irony that one of the most unlikely victims of the coronavirus was a beer that shared the same name. As the COVID-19 pandemic swept through the United States, sales of Corona beer plummeted.

By the end of February 2020, as the number of coronavirus cases rose globally, Corona became a popular topic for memes and videos on social media. Despite having no connection to the virus, online searches for "corona beer virus" and "beer coronavirus" increased.

According to YouGov, Corona's buzz score, which measures whether American adults have heard positive or negative things about the brand, fell from 75 to 51 since the beginning of the year.

Corona is owned by Anheuser-Busch InBev and Constellation Brands is the company that has exclusive perpetual brand license in the US to import, market and sell Corona. From February 21 to March 20, 2020, both companies' stock fell over 40% as investors feared, at least in part, that consumers would stop buying the beer brand that shared a name with the virus causing the pandemic.

5W Public Relations, one of the biggest independently-owned PR agencies in the United States, conducted a survey at the end of February, asking people about Corona beer. Some of their results:

• 38% of beer-drinking Americans would not buy Corona under any circumstances
• Among those who said they usually drink Corona, 4% said they would stop drinking Corona
• 14% said they wouldn't order Corona in a public venue
• 16% of beer drinking Americans were confused about whether Corona beer was related to the coronavirus

There was a 12% decline in revenue in the first half of 2020 compared to the same period the previous year, but surprisingly sales remained steady throughout the remainder of the year. Despite all of this, Corona remains the most valuable worldwide brand of beer, and the most popular beer in the United States.

People Panic Bought and Hoarded Toilet Paper

It was a strange sight to behold—hordes of people frantically pushing shopping carts through the aisles, throwing packs of toilet paper and bottles of hand sanitizer into their baskets as if their lives depended on it. The shelves that once held these mundane household items were now bare, stripped of their usual inventory.

This was the scene at supermarkets and pharmacies across the country as the COVID-19 pandemic began to sweep through the United States.

Why were toilet paper and hand sanitizer singled out, of all things? To understand this peculiar phenomenon, we must first examine the psychology of panic buying.

When faced with a crisis, our brains tend to go into survival mode. We become more risk-averse and prioritize the acquisition of resources that we believe will help us weather the storm. For some, this might mean stockpiling food and water. For others, it could mean buying face masks and hand sanitizer.

Toilet paper seemed to be a hot commodity during the early days of the pandemic. One theory suggests that people were buying up large quantities of it to feel a sense of control in an uncertain time. After all, there's something reassuring about having a well-stocked supply of toilet paper in your bathroom, even if you're not exactly sure why you need it.

But the demand for toilet paper far outstripped the supply, leading to shortages and even instances of hoarding. In some cases, people were spotted pushing shopping carts loaded with dozens of packs of toilet paper out of stores, leaving none for the rest of their communities.

This behavior was met with a mix of confusion and outrage from those who were unable to find the supplies they needed. Many took to social media to express their frustration, with the hashtag #toiletpaperpanic trending on Twitter.

The demand for hand sanitizer was also off the charts, as people sought to protect themselves from the highly contagious virus. Stores quickly ran out inventory, and prices for the remaining bottles appeared in large quantities on eBay, Amazon, and Facebook Marketplace.

In some cases, enterprising individuals saw an opportunity to make a quick buck by hoarding hand sanitizer and selling it at a markup. This only exacerbated the problem, as people were forced to pay exorbitant prices for a product that had previously been readily available.

As the pandemic wore on, it became clear that the panic buying of toilet paper and hand sanitizer was unfounded. These items can be useful in preventing the spread of germs, but there was no need to hoard them to the point of scarcity.

In fact, the World Health Organization (WHO) recommended a more holistic approach to preventing the spread of COVID-19, including washing hands frequently with soap and water, avoiding close contact with people who are sick, and wearing a mask in public.

The next time a crisis strikes, try to resist the urge to panic buy. Remember that hoarding supplies does more harm than good, and that there are more effective ways to protect yourself and your community.

Restaurants

Restaurants Recorded Contact Tracing Information While Checking Diners In

As restaurants started opening and people were allowed to dine indoors, one of the stipulations in some areas was that the restaurant was required to log their patron's information prior to seating them.

If it was reported that somebody who was dining at the restaurant had a case of COVID-19, the health department could trace the customer back to the restaurant and then could request the whole list of people that were dining in the restaurant the same day to alert them that they were in close contact.

In theory, that network was supposed to exist and be used in certain cases to prevent massive transmissions of the disease. In reality, the practice never really delivered on its promise to slow the spread of the disease.

Some restaurants found that people weren't happy giving up their information so freely. Many people looked at it as an invasion of privacy. People would offer obviously fake names and phone numbers, just to move past the hurdle and be seated.

Mostly, health departments didn't have the infrastructure in place to follow-up on every new case with an investigation and the proper connections they would have to make with the people who perhaps encountered the person who was infected.

While public health researchers were convinced indoor dining was a risky activity in areas where COVID-19 was spreading, getting solid data to justify restaurant restrictions was difficult. It takes in-depth, resource-heavy disease investigations to determine where people were exposed to the coronavirus, and those contact-tracing efforts never got off the ground in most of the country.

While restaurants appeared to be among the most common places to get infected with COVID-19, contact tracing in most areas had been so lackluster that few health departments have been able to link disease clusters to in-person dining.

Customers Were Required to Wear Masks While Walking to Table

Of all the things the public was asked to do during the pandemic to slow the spread of the disease, this one was among the most mocked and ridiculed. The policy was that while you were walking the 20 steps to your table, you had to keep your mask on your face.

However, as soon as you got to your table, you were free to take you mask off for the entire duration of your meal. It made no sense. Did the virus know you were standing or sitting? Was the 10 second walk riskier than the 45 minutes sitting at the table?

The logic didn't hold up for many people. Why go through the song and dance of having the mask on during the walk to the table but then be totally fine taking the mask off when you got to the table?

When patrons are seated, this is really when their mouth is doing the busy work. The eating, drinking, and speaking across the table is when the droplets really start flying! The walk to the table is quiet, single-file, and rapid. There is almost a zero percent chance of transmission during that part of the dining experience.

A lot of scientists felt out of the loop on this one. The rule appeared to be a half-measure which allowed the restaurants to be open. It gave the impression that a certain level of consideration was being given to COVID-19 transmission. Almost as if the people in charge were saying, "Yes, we know masks aren't doing any good, but if you want to still be able to dine out, you must still do what we say."

The people that complied with wearing masks on the way to the table didn't do it because they were afraid of getting sick (people that were afraid of getting sick rightfully stayed home). They wore the masks because they wanted to be out in a restaurant with friends and family and didn't want that privilege to be taken away again. The restaurant owners had the signs up because they didn't want to get a fine, as they were barely surviving as it was. They also didn't want to give the government any excuse to shut them down for not complying.

It was all just theater. The masks did nothing in this setting, they were just there for show. People willingly complied to keep the restaurants open and have the freedom to be out and about again.

Buffets Required Customers to Wear Gloves

Many states opened restaurants in phases. Full-service restaurants were allowed to open first, in reduced capacity. In a second phase, they were allowed to open with larger capacity. In this second phase, buffet-style restaurants were also allowed to open, with many safety protocols put in place.

Buffet-style restaurants, which allow customers to serve themselves from a selection of food, were considered high-risk for the transmission of COVID-19. With people coming into close contact with shared utensils and surfaces, there was a risk of the virus spreading from person to person.

For this reason, many buffet-style restaurants were forced to close their doors during the early days of the pandemic. For instance, Golden Corral shut down every single restaurant they run in 42 states. As the months wore on and the risk of transmission began to decrease, some of their restaurants were able to reopen with a few changes. They added contact tracing, and the restaurant were reconfigured to allow for social distancing. When it was time to serve the food, each customer was handed plastic gloves and a plate. The offerings were reduced, and some items were altogether eliminated. In some restaurants, they converted the self-serve model to cafeteria style, where an employee served the food to each patron.

While the requirement to wear gloves was met with some hesitation by the public, it seemed to be an effective measure in reducing the risk of transmission. And as the pandemic wore on, more and more buffet-style restaurants began to implement similar measures.

Not all buffet-style restaurants were able to weather the storm of the pandemic. Sweet Tomatoes (operating as Souplantation in southern California) was a popular chain of buffet-style restaurants. All 97 locations went out of business on May 7, 2020, in the face of declining sales and the challenges posed by the pandemic. The closure of Sweet Tomatoes was met with sadness by many customers, who had come to rely on the chain for its fresh and flavorful food. For the company, the decision to close was a necessary one in the face of the challenges posed by the pandemic.

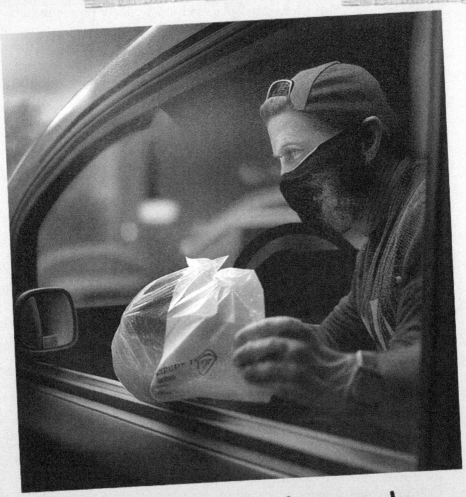

Fast Food Restaurants
Converted to Drive-thru Only

In the early days of the COVID-19 pandemic, fast food restaurants were faced with a difficult decision: how to continue serving customers while keeping everyone safe. Many chains decided to switch to drive-thru only service, a move that allowed them to maintain social distancing and minimize contact between employees and customers.

They limited contact by adding plexiglass barriers to their drive-thru windows, adopted wireless credit card readers with handles that they could extend out the window for customers to use themselves, and avoided hand-to-hand contact by passing food to customers in plastic tubs.

In March of 2020, the fast-food industry earned $8.3 billion in sales from drive-thrus, which was higher than the $8 billion in sales during the same period in 2019. Drive-thru sales accounted for approximately 70% of fast-food sales each month in May of 2020, according to the New York Times.

Drive-thrus were crucial lifelines for fast-food chains during the pandemic. Restaurants without drive-thrus had to shut down while others switched to a strictly drive-thru or curbside pickup model. Over 1,500 locations of chain restaurants, most of which lacked drive-thrus, were permanently closed due to the pandemic.

Quick service restaurants like Chipotle and Jimmy John's pivoted to a pickup only model. Customers used the apps to order their food, and then drove to the location to pick it up. In the dining room, all the tables and booths were taped off, and there were several racks of shelves, with bags of food waiting to be picked up, labeled with the customer's name, sorted by order time.

It was easy to imagine a future where these restaurants eliminated the indoor seating area altogether, and with it the expense of cleaning and maintaining the dining room and the bathrooms.

UberEats, GrubHub, and
DoorDash Sales Went Crazy

As the COVID-19 pandemic swept through the United States, one industry that saw a sudden and dramatic increase in demand was food delivery. Services like Grubhub, DoorDash, and Uber Eats experienced a surge in popularity as people looked for ways to have their meals delivered to their homes.

But why was there such a sudden surge in demand for food delivery? To understand this phenomenon, we must examine the changes that the pandemic brought about in our daily lives.

As the virus spread, people were advised to stay home and practice social distancing to slow its spread. This meant that restaurants were forced to close their doors or switch to takeout and delivery only.

At the same time, people were feeling anxious and uncertain about the future. The prospect of cooking meals from scratch was daunting, and people were flush with cash from the stimulus. The idea of leaving the house to go grocery shopping was unappealing.

Enter food delivery services. With the tap of a finger, people were able to have their favorite meals delivered straight to their doors. This convenience was particularly appealing to those who were working from home or had young children to care for.

The demand for food delivery was not limited to just restaurants. Grocery delivery services like Instacart also saw a surge in popularity, as people looked for ways to have their groceries delivered rather than risk going to the store in person.

For the food delivery companies, this sudden surge in demand was both a blessing and a curse. On one hand, they were seeing record levels of business, but as competitors entered the space, and it was a challenge to implement safety measures for everyone.

Despite these challenges, the food delivery industry was one of the bright spots in an otherwise bleak economic landscape. And as the pandemic ended, these services continued to be a popular choice for people looking for convenient and safe ways to have their meals delivered.

#SupportLocal Movement Kept
Restaurants Afloat

At the beginning of the pandemic, as restaurants were forced to close their doors or switch to takeout and delivery only, people across the country began to show their support for their favorite local spots in a variety of ways. The idea was that big chain restaurants probably had the capital in their organization to weather a short-term downturn in sales, but with razor-thin profits, most locally owned restaurants weren't likely to make it through without some additional support.

One of the most obvious ways people supported their local restaurants was by ordering takeout or delivery. With dine-in service no longer an option, many people turned to these options to enjoy the delicious food from their favorite spots while also helping to keep these businesses afloat. From sharing menus and delivery options on social media to leaving generous tips for the hardworking staff, people found creative ways to show their support. This whole idea was lauded online and the hashtag #SupportLocal swept across the country.

But the #SuppprtLocal movement wasn't just about the food. It was also about the sense of community that these businesses provide. If the choice is between supporting Pizza Hut or the local pizza place, people would pick the local business. Many people made a point of leaving positive reviews on social media or on review sites like TripAdvisor, Google, and Yelp, helping to spread the word about their favorite spots and encouraging others to give them a try.

In addition to ordering takeout and leaving reviews, there were many other ways that people supported their local restaurants. Some restaurants encouraged their customers to purchase gift cards to use later, providing a much-needed source of income for these businesses when they needed it the most. Some restaurants updated their menus to have options such as "Buy the kitchen staff a round" or added merchandise such as stickers or clothing to boost the ticket total. Others made donations to fundraisers or contributed to crowdfunding campaigns set up to help keep local restaurants afloat.

One of the most heartwarming aspects of the #SupportLocal movement was the way that people came together to show their support. From neighborhood groups organizing mass takeout orders to communities coming together to support beloved local spots, it was truly a time of solidarity and generosity.

Restaurants Promoted
Cocktails-To-Go Programs to
Boost Sales

During the beginning of the pandemic, people were ordering a ton of takeout or delivery food, but the biggest profit maker in restaurants had always been alcohol sales. Restaurants were losing out on profits because people couldn't order these. People's favorite bars were still sitting mostly dark and abandoned, unable to return to in-person crowds.

What was the answer for this issue? Restaurants and bars started offering cocktails-to-go programs to their menus.

Bars and night clubs used to be lively and inviting on weekends, but now they seem almost insignificant in their emptiness. However, some bars were able to adapt to the situation by providing takeout and delivery services to bring in enough money to stay afloat. Despite the widespread shutdowns of bars and restaurants in cities and states across the country, people still wanted to be able to get a drink from their favorite places. It took a lot of quick and collaborative work, but legislators were amazingly eager to help relax rules to allow establishments to add premixed drinks to the beer and wine offerings already available to customers' takeout or delivery orders.

One of the biggest advantages of cocktails to go was the convenience factor. No longer were people limited to the selection of beer and wine that most takeout and delivery restaurants offered—they could now enjoy their favorite delicious cocktails as well. And with many bars and restaurants offering pre-made mixes or easy-to-follow instructions, it was easier than ever to craft a delicious drink and bring a little bit of the bar experience right to the home.

The appeal of cocktails-to-go wasn't just about convenience, it was also about supporting the bars and restaurants that the community loved. Many of these businesses had been hit hard by the pandemic, and the ability to sell cocktails-to-go was a lifeline for many of them. By ordering a cocktail or two to take home, people were able to show their support and help keep these businesses afloat. The relaxed legislation was pretty much universally accepted and showed what could be done when people were working toward the same goal. The cocktails-to-go programs may be one of the ideas that survives the pandemic and becomes a staple in ordering takeout in the future.

Restaurants Moved Their Dining Rooms Outdoors

As the COVID-19 pandemic swept across the country, restaurants were forced to get creative to stay afloat. With indoor dining no longer an option in many places, and takeout and delivery only service proving to be a less-than-ideal solution for many businesses, many restaurants scrambled to add outdoor seating to continue serving customers while maintaining social distancing.

At first, the transition to outdoor seating seemed like a simple solution. After all, what could be more pleasant than dining al fresco on a warm summer evening? But as restaurants began to set up tables and chairs on sidewalks and in parking lots, they quickly discovered that the legalities of outdoor seating were anything but simple.

One of the biggest challenges restaurants faced was obtaining the necessary permits and approvals. In many cases, restaurants had to go through a lengthy and complex process to set up outdoor seating, including obtaining permission from the city or town in which they were located. With many municipalities overwhelmed by the pandemic and struggling to keep up with the demand for permits, the process of getting approved could take weeks or even months.

In addition to the challenges of obtaining permits, restaurants also had to deal with a host of other legalities when it came to outdoor seating. These included issues such as accessibility, fire safety, and the need to provide adequate lighting and heating for customers. And with many restaurants operating on tight budgets and with reduced staff, navigating these complex legal issues was a daunting task.

Despite these challenges, many restaurants were able to successfully add outdoor seating and continue serving customers during the pandemic. Through hard work and determination, they were able to overcome the legal and logistical hurdles and provide a safe and enjoyable dining experience for their customers.

Restaurants Got Creative With Special Seating Choices

As the pandemic continued, dining outdoors became a popular means of supporting local restaurants while also getting a change of scenery. However, with winter fast approaching in cities across North America, the Independent Restaurant Coalition warned that as many as 85% of independent restaurants could be lost by the end of 2020.

Restaurants needed a way to keep the outdoor dining trend going, but given the challenges posed by winter weather, there was a need to find ways to make outdoor dining both safe and comfortable, while also supporting the struggling restaurant industry.

In American cities where cold weather was approaching and outdoor dining had become crucial for restaurants struggling to survive during the pandemic, transparent dome-shaped structures began to appear to offer shelter and security for willing diners.

The units were efficient. They trapped heat and regulated the air so it wouldn't get too hot or stuffy inside. Each bubble accommodated only one table, so the bubbles were a a near perfect way to reduce a group's exposure to other individuals nearby.

Local governments loosened zoning restrictions early in the pandemic to provide a lifeline to restaurants and bars by allowing them to set up these impromptu pods, and restaurants eagerly snapped at the chance to provide safe options for their customers.

Due to concerns about eating maskless in poorly ventilated, potentially crowded dining rooms, many potential diners were understandably cautious. However, even as the weather changed, the al fresco option remained appealing, even in locations where it meant wearing warm clothing to eat outside.

While the country's pop-up street cafés were not intended to be a permanent solution, they have been one of the few measures to persist throughout the pandemic. People liked them, as they provided both a unique warm setting in the cold, and also a level of privacy, while making the group feel more secure.

Culture

Workers Were Classified As
Either Essential or
Non-essential

As governments around the world imposed lockdowns and restrictions on travel and activity, a distinction began to emerge between "essential" and "non-essential" workers.

Essential workers, as defined by the government, were those who provided vital services and were therefore allowed to continue working during the lockdown. These included healthcare workers, first responders, grocery store employees, and others who were deemed necessary for the maintenance of society.

Non-essential workers, on the other hand, were those whose jobs were not considered essential and were therefore required to stay home during the lockdown. These were more likely to be people who worked in offices, and blue collars workers in industries deemed less essential for our society.

For essential workers, the COVID-19 pandemic brought with it a host of challenges. These workers were often required to work long hours under difficult and stressful conditions, and they faced the risk of exposure to the virus daily.

To help essential workers navigate the restrictions and continue to do their jobs, many governments introduced special measures such as driving permits. These permits, which were often issued by local authorities, allowed essential workers to travel during the lockdown.

Some non-essential workers were furloughed or laid off, and they faced financial uncertainty and the possibility of long-term unemployment. Some also struggled with the isolation and boredom of being confined to their homes for long periods of time.

While the challenges faced by these two groups may be different, they were both facing unprecedented challenges because of the COVID-19 pandemic. Both essential workers risking their health to keep society running and non-essential workers trying to navigate financial and personal challenges during the lockdown, struggled to keep some normalcy in their lives.

Pedestrians Became Super Aware of Other Pedestrians

People across the globe scrambled to understand and respond to the crisis. Fear and uncertainty were rampant. Science was unsettled. And for many people, this fear manifested itself in strange ways.

Even in the lockdown period, people would still leave their houses to get some exercise, and of course dogs still needed to be walked. Sometimes people just needed to clear their minds and take a walk, especially those that were cooped up in their houses all day. But on their walk, they might encounter a neighbor who was also in that same mindset.

In a previous era, the friendly neighbor might have stopped and had a quick chat with their neighbor. To comment on what a beautiful day it was, how nice their lawn is looking, or other neighborly niceties. But one of the most common behaviors that emerged early on was for people to give other pedestrians wide berths when they encountered each other on the streets or sidewalks.

Whether it was out of a genuine concern for their own safety or simply a subconscious desire to avoid any unnecessary interactions, many people found themselves not wanting to be the person to create an uncomfortable situation, even if it meant crossing to the other side of the road to avoid confrontation altogether.

Even if one person was totally comfortable, they never knew how the other person would handle a stop and chat. The six-foot social distance rule was a guideline, but far from hard science early on. And if heaven forbid one of the people was wearing a mask while walking alone (yeah, that happened) it was almost like a big blinking billboard that said, "Leave me alone. Do not engage with me!"

For some people, the fear of encountering others during the pandemic was so strong that they went to extreme lengths to avoid it. This included wearing face masks and gloves in public, even when it was not required by law, and avoiding crowded areas altogether. For others, the fear was more subtle, manifesting itself in the way they interacted with others or in their body language. It was one of the new social cues that people had to learn during the start of the pandemic.

People Painted Rocks and Left Them On Paths for Others to Discover

As the COVID-19 pandemic swept across the country, many people found themselves feeling isolated and alone. With lockdowns and social distancing measures in place, it was harder than ever to connect with others and find a sense of community. But in the midst of all this fear and uncertainty, a small but heartwarming phenomenon began: painted rocks with positive messages popping up randomly in public spaces.

The trend started on TikTok, mostly by kids who were stuck at home and seeking an uplifting and fun art project. For all of the negativity that social media rightfully gets for being a cesspool, when something positive like this trends, it can be a beautiful thing.

These painted rocks, which were often decorated with bright colors and uplifting messages, seemed to appear out of nowhere, and they quickly became a source of joy and inspiration for many people. Some of the messages were simple and straightforward, such as "Stay strong" or "We're all in this together," while others were more creative and imaginative. No matter what the message, these painted rocks provided a much-needed reminder that we were all in this together and that there was hope and beauty to be found even in the darkest of times.

One of the most appealing aspects of the painted rocks trend was the element of surprise. People went about their daily lives and might stumble across one hidden in a park or tucked into a flowerpot, granting a moment of joy and connection that many people desperately needed. And as more and more people began to participate in the trend, the painted rocks became a way for people to connect with each other and share their own messages of hope and positivity.

As the pandemic dragged on and the painted rocks continued to appear, they became a symbol of the resilience and determination of the human spirit. Even in the face of unprecedented challenges, people found ways to come together and support each other, and the painted rocks were a small but powerful part of that.

Looking back on the beginning of the COVID-19 pandemic, it's clear that the painted rocks trend was a bright spot in an otherwise difficult and uncertain time. They provided a moment of joy and connection for many people, and they were a reminder that even in the darkest of times, there is always hope and beauty to be found.

Pet Owners Were Nervous About Pets Catching and Spreading Virus

As the COVID-19 pandemic swept across the country, many people found themselves becoming increasingly paranoid about the potential risks and dangers of the virus. And for some people, this paranoia extended to their beloved pets.

The Centers for Disease Control and Prevention (CDC) advised that people who were suspected or confirmed to have COVID-19 should abstain from interacting with animals, such as pets, livestock, and wildlife. COVID-19 infections have been reported in animals worldwide, with most contracting the virus from individuals with COVID-19, including owners, caregivers, or others with close contact. The complete list of animals that can be infected is still unknown, but documented cases include dogs and cats.

At the beginning of the pandemic, there was a lot of uncertainty about whether pets could contract or spread the virus, and this uncertainty led to some people taking extreme precautions to protect their furry friends. Some people went so far as to limit their pets' exposure to others, even going so far as to walk them at off-peak hours or in less crowded areas to minimize the risk of transmission.

Other people went even further, opting to isolate their pets completely and keep them at home for the duration of the pandemic. While this might have seemed like a safe and responsible thing to do, it came with its own set of challenges. For many people, their pets were an important source of companionship and support, and being separated from them for an extended period was a significant source of stress and anxiety.

Despite the uncertainty and paranoia surrounding pets and COVID-19, people needed reminding that the risk of transmission from pets to humans was generally considered to be low. While it was possible for pets to contract the virus, most cases involved close contact with infected humans, and the risk of transmission to humans through casual contact was minimal.

Consumers Turned to
Pre-prepared Food Meal Kits

In the United States, the pandemic led to increased interest in meal-kit delivery and recipe boxes, as families stayed at home and looked for convenient and healthy meal options. Meal-kit companies had been on the scene for about ten years before the pandemic, but the U.S. meal-kit market took off like crazy, growing over 68 percent, reaching $5.8 billion in 2020.

At the height of the pandemic, around 10 percent of Americans reported using a meal kit in the past 30 days, according to the market research firm NPD Group. The groups that were the most likely to use these meal prep kits were millennials and Generation Xers, especially those who lived in urban areas.

The pandemic provided a perfect storm of conditions for the meal-kit popularity surge. People had more disposable income, as the first $1,200 stimulus checks went out in April 2020. People had time on their hands, with many people working remotely, and not a lot of ways to spend disposable income with many entertainment options still locked down. Dining options were either limited or made people feel uneasy to be eating in restaurants.

Meal kits filled a gap in the market. These delivered boxes from companies like Hello Fresh, Sun basket and Blue Apron, would deliver the ingredients right to the door, with easy-to-follow recipes and delicious foods, that would allow families to try something new, while also having an activity to do in their homes.

Restaurants such as Chick-fil-A, Bob Evans, and Denny's also entered the meal-kit market, offering take home kits for families to prepare on their own, especially around holiday times, with turkey, ham and traditional holiday foods all packaged together. The popularity caused grocery stores like Kroger, Albertsons, Walmart, Whole Foods, and Publix to expand their offerings in the deli and freezer aisles.

Meal kits were a way to try new recipes and improve cooking skills. Others found meal kits helpful in reducing decision-making fatigue and keeping their children satisfied with dinner options. It was a fun way to stay home and eat delicious food during the pandemic.

People Started Greeting Each Other With Elbow Bumping or Foot Tapping

During the pandemic, people adopted practices that minimize human contact to prevent the spread of the disease. Social distancing became the norm, and alternative greetings such as fist bumping, waving, bowing, foot tapping, and elbow bumping replaced handshakes.

Handshakes have a long history and are a universal symbol of greeting, respect, congratulations, and farewell. However, adherence to hand hygiene guidelines was often lacking, and experts warned that handshakes can transfer many bacteria and pathogens.

Of these alternatives, the fist bump is the closest motion to a traditional handshake, and transmits fewer pathogens compared to a handshake or high five. The fist bump maintained the essential qualities of a handshake by using the upper extremity and allowing eye contact, while it also reduced the risk of contamination that came with the filthy inside of the hand. But for some, that was still too much skin-to-skin contact.

Elbow bumping became a popular way to greet others, with prominent figures such as political leaders, health officials, and athletes adopting this practice as a safer alternative to traditional forms of greeting.

At the very beginning of March 2020, Vice President Mike Pence, who was tasked by the Trump administration to lead the U.S. response to the coronavirus pandemic, demonstrated this trend by using an elbow bump to greet Governor Jay Inslee during his visit to Washington state. The US Women's National Soccer Team traded elbows instead of handshakes in a match with England, and baseball players opted for this celebration over the traditional high five in spring training. People were quick to follow the trend, and the elbow bump took off.

More coordinated and paranoid people took it one step further (pun intended), by replacing the handshake with the footshake. This greeting did away with upper body connection altogether, instead bringing the inside of each person's right foot together to tap, sometimes followed up with the left feet tapping. This one took a bit more balance and looked a little silly. It didn't quite catch on as well as the elbow bump.

Parades Banned Throwing Candy to Children

By the summer parade season hit in 2020, the United States was well within the throes of the pandemic. Children had been coping with the impact of the pandemic for a significant period, with cancelled Easter egg hunts, spring sports, and end-of-school-year events.

With summer vacation underway, many were now grappling with the prospect of celebrating the Fourth of July without traditional festivities such as fireworks, parades, ball games, and parties, many of which were called off due to restrictions on the number of people who could get together.

The Centers for Disease Control and Prevention emphasized the importance of social distancing during the Fourth of July holiday, given recent surges in COVID-19 cases, and urged families to celebrate in a safe manner.

For the parades that still were allowed to happen, they were drastically reimagined. Most places banned one of the most popular parts of a parade, candy throwing. The thinking was that if someone who is sitting on the back of 1962 Ford Thunderbird grabs a handful of Starbursts and Skittles and throws it into the crowd, who knows what the hell could happen?

Kids were all still allowed to go to the store and buy their own candy. It's not like candy sale were banned in any way. If we were worried about the person throwing the candy, we could have passed around Purell before the parade started. If kids running out into the street together broke the six-foot bubble, well, kids never really respected that rule to begin with—they are kids. In fact, the most dangerous part of throwing the candy would have been a foot getting ran over by the parade float, or getting run into by a Shriner's go-kart (too soon?). Instead, candy tossing was banned. Because it's just good science.

Other places adopted reverse parades, where the floats were stationary, and families would drive through them very slowly, but stay in their own cars. Although this was different from the usual festivities, it still provided a fun way to celebrate the holiday. You could tell who the most invested parents were because they threw candy to their kids in the back seat.

Receptionist Areas Started Putting Out Clean and Used Pen Cups

During the pandemic, a host of new behaviors and protocols emerged as people searched for ways to reduce the risk of transmission, especially when it came to shared surfaces.

One shared surface that is everywhere from doctor's offices, to banks, to the DMV, to school receptionist areas, was the pen. Gone were the days of the single pen tethered to a desk with the mighty chain. A chain so mighty it could stop even the most eager kleptomaniac from pocketing a free Bic. In the era of coronavirus, that pen was more dangerous than the intentions of the would-be thief looking to steal it.

With the risk of transmission from surface contact still a concern, pens became a source of anxiety for many people, who were worried about the risk of contamination from touching the same surface as others. For some, the solution was simple: bring your own pen with you everywhere you go. The problem was solved.

For the rest of the population who didn't carry a purse or pocket protector, we still needed somebody to provide for us. Some establishments replaced the one single pen on a chain with a whole new pen operation.

There were two jars, one marked very vividly 'Clean Pens' and it held more pens than you could ever steal in a lifetime. On the other side of the desk, far enough away that even the Carl Lewis of COVID-19 viruses couldn't jump across, was the "Dirty Pens" jar. This is where pens would go when it was time to visit the big ink well in the sky. A visitor would take a pen from the clean jar, write down the time, the date, check a couple boxes, scribble their signature, and then cast that pen to its death. Or so it seemed.

Whatever became of the "Dirty Pens"? Who among us witnessed what happened when the "Clean Pens" jar got depleted? Maybe the receptionist painstakingly rubbed down each pen with a Lysol wipe. Maybe box after box of brand new single-use pens were getting dumped in the landfill. Or maybe, she waited until no one was looking, and just swapped the pens back to the "Clean Pens" jar without giving it a second thought. Similar to how your favorite Italian restaurant takes uneaten bread and serves it in a new basket to the next table. We may never know.

People Weirdly Drive Around Alone Wearing a Face Mask (or Two!)

We all saw these people during the pandemic, driving around wearing a face mask (or maybe two), all alone in their cars, driving, completely masked up.

Most Americans recognized the importance of wearing face masks in crowded indoor spaces. They may not have even agreed with the policy, but they went along with it to be good citizens. But this question vexed so many people: why are these people driving around alone with a mask on? Once and for all, here are the best guesses:

The most common reason was that they were driving to or from a place where a mask was required, such as work or a crowded store. Some people kept their masks on while running errands to avoid repeatedly putting it on and taking it off between locations. Others who had absentminded tendencies conditioned themselves to always wear it. If you always have it on, you can't forget to put it on.

Face masks also served to keep faces warmer in colder months while waiting for the car to heat up for a few minutes in the bitter cold. Hot recycled breath was way warmer than the freezing cold air of a winter car sitting outside.

Perhaps the car was being used for a rideshare service, and you just missed the Uber or Lyft sticker? Drivers for these companies were required to have a mask on the whole time they were driving. In fact, their driver app monitored their face and could tell if the driver wasn't wearing a mask. The driver may have had a bag of food to deliver and his company mandated that the driver must wear a mask for deliveries.

Perhaps they had just robbed a bank and the car was stolen and they didn't want to get caught on traffic cameras. Ok, that one is far-fetched. But this is probably the most likely one:

They wear that mask just to confuse or piss other people off. That's right, it's a deliberate attempt to irritate others, and to cause controversy, maybe even to the point where they write a book about it and make it into a chapter. These people would get off on that idea.

People Handed Out Trick or Treating Candy Using Candy Chutes

One of the beloved holidays for children in the United States is Halloween. They look forward to it for months, picking out their costumes, making crafts and decorations in school, and of course, the night of trick-or-treating, which brings in a massive haul of candy.

Across the United States, large community events, parades, outdoor festivals, haunted houses, and corn mazes were canceled or altered in response to the pandemic. If there was a large gathering involved, chances were good that they were shut down or severely limited.

And in some areas, cities and states tried to do the unthinkable: ban neighborhood trick-or-treating altogether.

Los Angeles County health officials in California gained attention for being among the first to introduce new rules and regulations for Halloween. According to the Los Angeles Times, officials attempted to enforce a complete prohibition on trick-or-treating, citing the difficulty of maintaining safe social distancing if everyone took to the streets at the same time. Less than a day later, after people revolted, the ban was lifted. You can't stop kids from trick-or-treating.

Trick-or-treating was a no-brainer perfect pandemic-proof activity for the kids. Even for the hyper-paranoid parents, they could still have their kids wear a face mask underneath or as part of their costume—doctors/nurses, monsters, and superheroes all wear masks—and most kids have on gloves for the chilly night anyway. What could be the harm sending the kids out on their favorite night?

Some people got clever with the ways that they handed out candy. The "Please Take One" sign next to the bowl of peanut butter cups was especially popular in the pandemic, as people handing out candy wanted to limit their exposure as well. That sign was especially ignored by the greediest of our masked children that year.

Another ingenious idea was the use of candy chutes, made from cardboard tubes or PVC pipes, that allowed people to slide their candy down to trick-or-treaters while maintaining distance. There was one thing for absolute certain about kids on Halloween: they don't care how the candy winds up in their bag, just so long as it does.

Public Libraries Closed But Offered Pickup Times for Books

Public libraries were not immune to the problems of the pandemic. Forced to close or reduce visitations throughout the year, they faced immense pressure to prioritize the health and safety of their staff and patrons, while still maintaining services. Despite these challenges, many libraries exhibited remarkable ingenuity. They developed new programs and services quickly, adapted to shifting circumstances dynamically, and partnered with community organizations to enhance access to their resources, whether in person or virtually.

Most public libraries in the United States made changes to their policies, including extending online renewals so their patrons wouldn't have to risk exposures to return books or extend checkout periods during surges in cases. Leaders redirected their budgets quickly, expanding online services for e-books, and streaming media, rather than physical media. They also had to cancel a lot of their in-person learning and educational offerings due to restrictions, but pivoted to adding virtual learning classes online.

Some libraries that had access to 3D printers used their resources to print face shields for local regional hospitals that needed additional personal protective equipment.

Public libraries provide the only means of free access to computers and the internet for over 20 million individuals without home broadband. In a single year, public libraries host almost 258 million computer sessions. However, the closure of library buildings due to the pandemic resulted in many not having access. During lockdowns, many libraries left their public Wi-Fi accessible despite the library building being closed. Many more increased their signals or offered hotspot hardware as an item that could be checked out.

Some libraries had pickup times available. Their patrons could checkout their books and other media on the website, and then stop by the library. While nobody was allowed in during the lockdowns, staff would have the materials ready to be picked up, outside, at certain scheduled times.

Our public library system is one of the greatest treasures our society has, and during the pandemic, they stepped up as much as any other entity to help the public.

People Celebrated Their Birthdays With Drive-By Parties

For those whose birthday fell around the beginning of the pandemic, it was a big old bummer. People genuinely felt bad and wanted to do something—anything—special for the birthday boy or girl.

The phenomenon of drive-by birthdays was created as stay-at-home orders were implemented and social distancing measures were put in place. People were forced to find new and creative ways to celebrate special occasions, such as birthdays. The drive-by birthday party was one such solution.

The idea was simple, ingenious, and heart-warming at the same time. Just like a regular party, invitations were sent out. The planner would coordinate a time and invited friends and family would gather in their cars at a predetermined spot, around the corner from the birthday person's house. Vehicles would stage up and wait until everyone arrived. Then, in a big, long parade, the well-wishers would all drive by the birthday person's house, honking, waving, and holding up signs to wish them a happy birthday, while the birthday person would sit out in their front yard, receiving all the attention and love from the passing by vehicles.

Some people even decorated their cars with streamers and balloons to make the occasion more festive. People could hand their cards and gifts out their windows, sometimes placing the cards in a mailbox and gifts on a table. But nobody made physical contact with each other. It was an efficient way to show somebody they were special without breaking any social distancing rules.

One thing that made drive-by birthdays so special was the sense of community and togetherness they fostered. Despite being physically separated from one another, people were still able to come together and show their love and support for their friends and families.

The drive-by birthday trend also had the added benefit of providing a much-needed break from the monotony of quarantine life. For many people, the daily routine of staying at home had become quite tedious, and the excitement and novelty of a drive-by birthday party provided a welcome change of pace. It was as fun for the people driving by as the person sitting in their front yard.

Friends and Families Moved Their Get-Togethers to the Outdoors

Throughout the pandemic, experts consistently told us that the science was clear: the risk of contracting the virus was significantly lower outdoors than indoors. If individuals wanted to socialize with friends, which some people absolutely did, shifting the gathering outside would decrease their chances of contracting COVID-19.

People were forced to find new and creative ways to socialize with friends and family while still maintaining social distance. The trend became outdoor gatherings. People would still get together, but instead of playing cards or watching the big game indoors, they would take their conversations and activities outside, around a bonfire, or spread out casually in lawn chairs in their backyards with a projector showing a movie or a sporting event.

The great outdoors became the new spot for catching up with friends. Parks and backyards were filled with people sitting on blankets, enjoying picnics, and having conversations at a safe distance. Others organized outdoor contactless games like soccer to have some physical activity and spend time together.

Outdoor gatherings were considered lower risk because of many factors. Wind could disperse viral droplets, reducing the chances of transmission. Sunlight could also kill some of the virus, further lowering the risk. Being outdoors in open spaces prevented the virus from accumulating in concentrated amounts, which could happen in indoor spaces when infected individuals exhale in a confined area for prolonged periods of time. As a result, spending time outside with others was a safer option for socializing during the COVID-19 pandemic.

There was also the concept of defined social circles and keeping those circles tight. If your family was always hanging around with one other family, getting those two families together was safer because you could more easily track everyone's day-to-day general exposures. Once people from several different households came together, the risk of someone spreading the virus went up. Public health officials warned people to keep the get togethers small and control the guest lists. This was a great reason to not invite unwanted guests over to the party.

People Would Have to Visit
Their Loved Ones Thru Closed
Windows

Since late March 2020, nursing homes and assisted-living facilities across the country prohibited visitors. The population in the facilities was the most prone to the virus and an outbreak could cause serious devastation to the population. In most states, people contracting the virus in long-term care facilities accounted for most of the deaths from COVID-19. This meant that many families were unable to see or communicate with their elderly loved ones in person, for weeks or months on end.

One of the most difficult challenges faced by many families was the need to keep elderly loved ones safe by avoiding in-person visits. Families had to drop off care packages at locked doors and wave to their loved ones from afar. Most resorted to communication through remote video conferencing, which presented challenges with an elderly population.

Around mid-June 2020, many states loosened the guidelines and allowed for window visitations, provided protocols were followed. It was a way to connect with their elderly loved ones, while keeping them safe.

Window visits involved meeting up, with the resident sitting safely inside, and the visitors outside, with a window between that provided a barrier for transmission. The family members could talk on the phone to hear better, but the face-to-face contact was important.

Some families gathered outside of the building, brought signs, balloons, and even set up speakers so they could play music to the residents inside. Others would simply stand outside a window and have a conversation with their loved one, even if it was through glass.

This was one of the first instances where lockdown measures were relaxed, and it's helped alleviate the seclusion felt by seniors. Research showed that prolonged isolation could lead to a decline in life expectancy and an increased risk of heart disease and dementia. It also made it easier for family members to keep tabs on the resident's wellbeing and ensure their daily necessities were met. It brightened up the day for the elderly person and their caretakers and provided a sense of connection for the visitors. Families got to reconnect in a time when nursing homes were heavily locked down.

People Let Their Mail and Packages Sit Outside and Wiped Them Down

One of the popular themes during the coronavirus pandemic was overkill, and how people managed their own behaviors. From the earliest news of the virus, the direction given to people from the science community shifted, and how people adapted to that new information showed a lot about their personality.

For instance, at the very beginning, health officials knew less about the ways the virus spread, and people decided it was a good idea to let their mail and packages sit outside for an extra-long period of time. The sun and the environment would kill the virus and reduce the potential for spreading. Then, when they finally brought them inside, they wiped them down with disinfectant spray or wipes.

However, the science became well-established that the primary mode of transmission was through respiratory droplets emitted during activities such as talking, coughing, sneezing. Officials emphasized the need for wearing masks and practicing social distancing.

While it was still recommended to clean frequently touched surfaces, it was important to remember that viruses do not jump off surfaces to infect people. For an infection to occur, there needs to be enough surviving virus on the surface, the person must touch it with their hands, and then touch their mouth, nose, or eyes. Therefore, excessive disinfecting may have diminishing returns, particularly if people practice good hand washing habits.

Public health officials faced a challenge in advising people on the appropriate level of cleaning required, particularly if cleaning did not cause any harm. Technically, wiping down your Amazon package didn't hurt anything, but it really didn't help anything, either.

While regular surface disinfection may not have significantly decreased the risk of COVID-19 transmission, it did provide a sense of control for individuals when they felt powerless. They couldn't control a lot of what was happening in the world, but they could definitely spray their mail down with disinfectant spray, and that gave them the feeling of control. Clorox Co.'s business unit that manufactures cleaning products experienced a 30% surge in sales in 2020, and that must have felt pretty good for that company as well.

Friends Got Together With Zoom Happy Hours

In the beginning of 2020, things started deteriorating rapidly. By the end of January, China had locked down Wuhan, a city of 11 million people and the United States had issued a travel ban directed at people coming over from China. By the end of February, cases were popping up all over the country, and on February 29, the first fatality was reported in Kirkland, WA.

By March 11, the total deaths had jumped to 37. Schools and colleges were shutting down in-person classes or canceling the remainder of the semester, the NBA suspended their season, and cities, counties and states started issuing bans on large numbers of people gathering.

This was around the time employers started sending their employees home. The virus was the number one topic of discussion in the workplace. Every meeting began with, "Did you hear that (fill in the blank) is closing?" and the break room was full of speculation about what was coming next. During that week, many employees grabbed their laptops, maybe an external monitor, and headed out of the office for what would turn out to be a very long time.

After about two weeks of working, most people had settled into a home-based routine. Wake up, settle into their home office, remotely log in and get some productive time in, switch over to read favorite news outlet website, scroll social media for updates from friends and family, make some lunch, check some emails, join the governor's daily livestream briefing talking about "flattening the curve", send a couple more emails, and then crack a hard seltzer and log off for the day.

It was a weird time. It was a scary, constantly evolving situation, with many unknowns. People didn't know the intricacies of how the disease spread and how people with preexisting conditions were more susceptible to succumbing from it.

There was also the uncertainty of life. Are the kids going to finish the school year? Should we cancel summer vacation plans? Am I a full-time remote employee now? Would things return to "normal" ever again?

One element of daily life that was missing was social interaction. Most people stayed home and stopped seeing friends and family in person. They interacted through remote video chats with coworkers during the workday, but once they logged out for the day, remaining at home made people feel isolated and lonely. Enter one of the silliest and most fun parts of the pandemic: the Zoom Happy Hour!

Invitations went out:

"Friday night - 7:00 pm - ? Let's tip one or two (or three) back and vent together about how much Covid sucks!

Click here to join."

And people DID join, in very large numbers*. Adults huddled together in front of their laptop or iPads sipping their favorite adult beverages, while squinting at a dozen small rectangles filled with the faces of friends and family staring back at them.

They discussed the craziness of the day's news, personal anecdotes from being out and about in the pandemic, and hopefully just made each other laugh and smile and forget about their uneasiness.

These calls sometimes went all night. Depending on the circle of friends, people would jump in and out of the call from different time zones throughout the call. It was fun to see old friends pop into the call and give an update from a different state.

At the end of the day, beating the boredom and breaking the monotony of being isolated at home was the main motivator for these virtual get togethers. Plenty of laughs were had and stress relieved and a little bit of normalcy was returned.

By the way, the whole activity was "Zoom Happy Hour" and wasn't "Microsoft Teams Happy Hour" or "Google Hangouts Happy Hour". During this period, "Zoom" was both both a proper company name and it was so popular that it replaced the generic term "video chat", the same way people call any facial tissue "Kleenex" even if it's not that brand. The popularity of Zoom software soared, as did the value of the company. The stock price for Zoom rose over 700% from the beginning of 2020 to its peak in October. That was just one of the thousands of topics that were discussed on the happy hour calls.

Politics

The Government Handed Out
Stimulus Checks and People
Went Nuts

In late March 2020, Congress passed the $2 trillion Coronavirus Aid, Relief, and Economic Security (CARES) Act, which provided $1,200 to individuals and $2,400 to married couples, with an additional $500 per child. It was followed by two more installments of pandemic relief being passed, later in 2020 and then again in 2021.

In fact, the government sent out around 472 million stimulus payments. Collectively, these payments had a total value of around $803 billion. Eligibility was phased out for those earning above certain thresholds. If the idea was to help people get some money pumping into the economy, it worked. People eagerly spent the money, like it was on fire.

On average, Americans spent roughly 1/3 of their first checks within 10 days of receiving it. For some, the money was to cover the essentials, catching up on rent and bills that had gone past due, as well as groceries. In April, the unemployment rate went up to 14.7 percent, and people struggled to make ends meet without an income.

Others used it to pay off debt or to make repairs to their homes or set up home offices. Some people used the stimulus money to make big purchases, such as new automobiles or RVs. People also used the stimulus money to support local businesses by buying gift cards or making other purchases. Some restaurants saw their sales go up 300% or higher the week that the first checks were sent out.

Others used it to invest in the stock market or to put money into savings. Broker Charles Schwab opened 609,000 new accounts in Q1, and Robinhood, a popular trading app with younger people, saw its daily trades in March jump up 300% from 2019. With all the new buyer demand, the market jumped 35% from end of March to May.

While the stimulus program was widely credited with providing much-needed financial assistance to many Americans during a difficult time, criticisms of the program were made that the amount was not enough and some needier people should have received more. Others thought that it was an irresponsible mismanagement of money that was bound to lead to high levels of inflation, which it did. When people on both sides of the aisle get upset, it usually means that the program was either very good, or very bad. We will have to wait to find out if there are lasting implications to our economy.

Paycheck Protection Program Loans Kept Businesses Operational

The Paycheck Protection Program (PPP) was a federal loan program that was created in response to the economic impact of the COVID-19 pandemic. The program was designed to provide small businesses with financial assistance to help cover their payroll and other expenses, such as rent and utilities.

The PPP loans were provided by banks and other lending institutions and were backed by the Small Business Administration (SBA). Eligible small businesses could apply for the loan, which could be for up to 2.5 times their average monthly payroll costs.

One of the key features of the PPP loans was that they could be forgiven if certain conditions were met. Specifically, if the loan proceeds were used for eligible expenses such as payroll, rent, and utilities, and at least 60% of the loan was used for payroll, the loan could be forgiven.

To apply for a PPP loan, small businesses had to provide documentation such as payroll records, tax forms, and other financial information to the lender. The lender would then review the application and, if approved, provide the loan to the business.

The PPP loan program was rolled out quickly and its goal was to keep the companies operational to avoid layoffs and keep the economy going. To that end, it was a very successful program, especially given how quickly it was rolled out. But it also had some limitations, and in some cases the loan application process and funds distribution was overwhelming to some small business owners.

To nobody's surprise, there was a lot of fraud involved. In fact, The New York Times cited a paper that said over 15% of PPP loans displayed indicators of possible fraud. Of the 11.8 million loans granted by the PPP, approximately 1.8 million exhibited signs of fraudulent activity. Their calculations suggested that approximately $76 billion of PPP loan funds were acquired through illicit means, which accounts for nearly 10% of the program's total budget of nearly $800 billion. Cynical people point to a government program which was that large and set up that fast and view a 10% fraud rate as a pretty low number, all things considered.

Black Lives Matter Protests Were Acceptable Social Gatherings

During the pandemic, health experts strongly advised against certain actions, such as having students in classrooms, attending religious services in person, visiting sick relatives in hospitals, and participating in large public gatherings.

When conservative anti-lockdown protesters gathered at state capitols around the country in April and May, these experts accordingly criticized their irresponsible, large-scale gatherings, and predicted that their actions would lead to a surge in new infections.

However, following the killing of George Floyd by police in Minneapolis on May 25, a massive protest movement erupted across the country, with tens of thousands of people taking to the streets. In a marked shift, over 1,300 public health officials expressed their support for the protests in a letter, and many participated in them.

Many people were left questioning whether their advice during the pandemic was sound after seeing such a turnabout. One minute they were condemning any large-scale group activity, and the next they completely signed off on the activity, if they supported the cause.

The letter that was signed took a firm stance and dismissed their colleagues who didn't agree, stating that the country faced a clear moral decision and that they must support the right of these protesters, despite potential risks of spreading the coronavirus. They drew a distinction between the anti-lockdown protestors and Black Lives Matter protesters. The letter asserted that individuals who protested stay-at-home orders on the steps of their state capitol buildings were motivated by white nationalism. Conversely, they declared that those protesting systemic racism needed to be supported. These public health advocates did not regard these second type of gatherings as too high-risk for COVID-19 spreading, but rather, they endorsed them as crucial to national public health. They reasoned that African Americans being killed by police was more a danger to their lives than contracting COVID-19 at a rally.

While there was no real data that showed either the anti-lockdown protests or the Black Lives Matter protests led to any spikes in cases, it was interesting to see some in the scientific community expose their true motives. The science didn't really matter quite as much as their political ideologies.

Justice System Decided to Release Certain Inmates from Prison

The Coronavirus Aid, Relief, and Economic Security (CARES) Act enabled the Justice Department to release individuals from federal prisons and place them on home confinement to safeguard those who were most susceptible to COVID-19 during the pandemic. As a result of this provision, over 11,000 people were released from federal prisons. This stemmed from five inmates dying from Covid-related illnesses in Ohio and Louisiana. Prisoners were considered based on their age, health, and length of remaining sentence.

To understand the reasoning of the moment, here is a letter from Bill Cosby's attorney, from March 2020, on why he should be released:

> I'm very concerned for Mr. Cosby's health in prison during the Coronavirus epidemic. The reason: Mr. Cosby is elderly and blind — and always needs to be escorted around the prison by support service inmates.
>
> Those inmates could fall victim to the Coronavirus and easily spread the disease to Mr. Cosby as they wheel him around in a wheelchair. Among their duties, the inmates bring Mr. Cosby to the infirmary for appointments and clean his cell.
>
> In addition, Mr. Cosby is constantly in contact with the correction officers who could contract the disease on the outside and bring it inside the prison, potentially exposing Mr. Cosby to the virus. Prisons and jails around the country are becoming infested with Coronavirus cases — and it's only a matter of time before Mr. Cosby's prison likely falls victim to the virus.
>
> For the record, Mr. Cosby has not been tested for the virus — but is feeling fine — other than being blind and his blood pressure spiking at times.

Cosby was indeed *not* eligible for release, as he was convicted of a violent offense and was deemed a sexual violent predator. But he *was* released in July 2021, when a judge threw out his conviction due to issues with his prosecution. So don't shed a tear for America's Dad.

Politicians Caught Going Against Their Own Social Distancing Guidelines

It's truly a sight to behold when our leaders practice what they preach. And during the COVID-19 pandemic, there was nobody louder or more sanctimonious at preaching than Speaker of the House Nancy Pelosi, House Representative Alexandria Ocasio-Cortez, and California Governor Gavin Newsom. As it turned out, they weren't quite as good at the practicing part.

It turned out that some of our nation's most vocal supporters of COVID-19 regulations and guidelines were caught breaking those very same rules they made sure everyone else was following.

Take for example, Nancy Pelosi. She previously advocated a nationwide mask mandate and criticized President Donald Trump for not wearing his mask in public. In September 2020, she was caught on camera breaking San Francisco's rule banning indoor hair salons, and she wasn't wearing her mask at the time. She plead ignorant to the rule and said she went by what the stylist told her was acceptable.

Meanwhile, in December 2021, Rep. Alexandria Ocasio-Cortez who staunchly supported mask and vaccine mandates and railed publicly on how irresponsible Florida was being by loosening their restrictions, was seen having a maskless meal in Florida, an irony that was not lost on Florida Governor Ron DeSantis. He couldn't resist when he tweeted:

> "Welcome to Florida, AOC! We hope you're enjoying a taste of freedom here in the Sunshine State".

And finally, California Governor Gavin Newsom, who pushed for the most restrictive state rules and Covid closures, also got busted. In November 2020, he was caught breaking one of his own rules he pushed for, by dining with a large group of friends at The French Laundry, one of the swankiest restaurants in the country.

Newsom was criticized for the dinner, and eventually was recalled as governor. He apologized soon after the photos surfaced, saying he needed "to preach and practice, not just preach and not practice."

For these politicians, the policy remained, "Rules for thee, not for me."

Mail-in Voting Movement Grew as Voters Avoided Polling Stations

The year of 2020 wasn't just a very notable one because of the pandemic, it was also a voting year. At the federal level alone there were 435 seats up for grabs in the House of Representatives, 33 open seats in the Senate, and of course, incumbent Donald Trump was defending his position as President of the United States from challenger Joe Biden. This was a big year for people to hit the polls.

But for many, they were still afraid or hesitant to go public venues. They were concerned with the increased risk of exposure while waiting in lines and sharing surfaces with others around the polls.

Across the nation, states and municipalities sought to protect the health and safety of voters. They made modifications to voting methods, resulting in a wide range of ballot casting options that differed significantly from one state to another.

While some states adhered to conventional voting procedures, others offered early voting opportunities and distributed mail-in ballots to all registered voters. Many made changes to their election laws, such as waiving the requirement for a notary or witness signature on ballots.

As a result, in the 2020 election, nearly 69% of voters across the country chose to vote non-traditionally, either through early voting or mail-in ballots, before Election Day. Nearly four-in-ten absentee or mail voters (39%) say they had never voted by this method prior to this November's election. Partially due to divisive politics, but mainly due to the ease of voting rules, this election featured the largest increase in voters between two presidential elections on record, with 17 million more people voting than in 2016.

The mail-in voting movement was met with mixed reactions. Some advocated for it to increase voter access and participation while ensuring public health and safety. Others raised concerns about potential voter fraud and the risk of ballots getting lost in the mail.

The 2020 election will be remembered as a unique event due to the occurrence of a pandemic. Judging by the popularity of mail-in voting ballots, this trend is expected to continue in future elections and is not going away anytime soon.

Healthcare

Vaccine Card Was Too Large to Fit into Wallets

Almost as soon as the COVID-19 virus was detected, the world's smartest vaccine researchers began working on the vaccine to stop the spread and eliminate the side effects of the disease. Operation Warp Speed (OWS) was announced May 15, 2020. It was a $10 billion public–private partnership initiated by the United States government to facilitate and accelerate the development, manufacturing, and distribution of COVID-19 vaccines.

The program promoted mass production of multiple vaccines, and different types of vaccine technologies. As soon as clinical trials confirmed one or more of the vaccines were successful, it would allow for super-fast distribution of the vaccines. By November 9, a phase 3 study showed one of the vaccines was over 90% effective in preventing COVID-19. It was time to get it to the people.

The first vaccine became available for individuals 16 years of age and older on December 11. The idea was getting one shot would be a start, and a second shot would increase the effects of the vaccine, and perhaps even more booster shots to shore up the effectiveness, depending on how the disease and variants evolved.

Meanwhile, in the ramp-up to deliver the vaccines, the CDC oversaw producing a method to track who had a vaccination and a way to quickly prove it, if need be. Enter the vaccination card. The card was supposed to be available to everyone to have and keep track of their own shots and side effects they experienced.

However, many people found that the vaccine cards were quite large, making them difficult to carry around in a purse or wallet. People would have to either fold them or carry them loosely in their pockets. This inconvenience caused some individuals worry about losing the card, or not carrying them when it was required to present them.

Why didn't they make the cards the size of a traditional ID card or a credit card, that would universally fit in any wallet? Eventually, the proof of vaccine went digital and ended up on people's phones, and it became less and less important to carry with you. The lesson was, the CDC does a lot of things well, but don't put them in charge of designing a piece of print material.

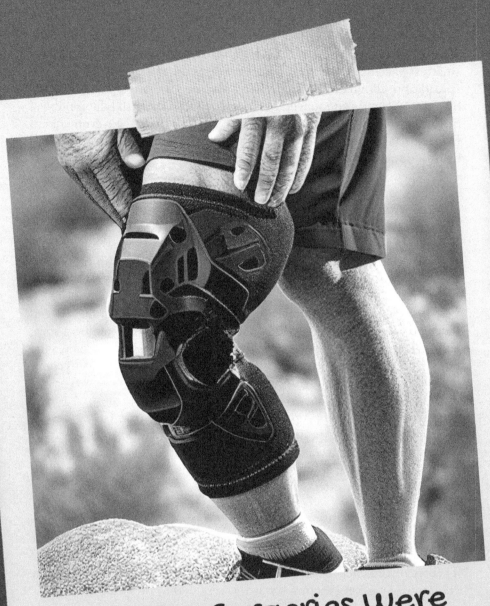

Elective Surgeries Were
Put Off to Keep
Hospital Beds Open

The pandemic had a profound impact on the medical industry. It affected not only patients who had COVID-19, but anybody else who was relying on the hospital for their medical needs.

During the COVID-19 pandemic, many elective surgeries of all kinds were put on hold to preserve hospital resources, protect health care workers and patients, and reduce the risk of further spread of the virus. This was a common decision made by many health systems and governments across the country.

This decision was made in response to the surge of COVID-19 patients requiring hospitalization and the need to reserve hospital beds, personal protective equipment (PPE), and medical staff for the treatment of COVID-19 patients. The suspension of elective surgeries was also intended to reduce the exposure of patients to crowded hospital environments.

As a result, many patients who were scheduled for elective surgeries such as knee or hip replacements, cataract removal, hernia repairs, and cosmetic procedures were asked to delay their surgeries until further notice. This was a difficult decision for many patients, as it caused delays in necessary medical treatments, and it caused significant disruptions to the usual care.

While delaying non-essential or elective procedures was useful in maintaining crucial healthcare resources during the COVID-19 response, the healthy officials acknowledged that prolonged postponements of certain medical care could pose significant risks to patients. These procedures were often necessary to manage chronic pain and illnesses, or to prevent, cure, or slow down disease progression. It was a difficult balancing act between prioritizing COVID-19 response and preparedness, and making sure the rest of the population was receiving timely and adequate health care.

While nobody was happy while they were in pain, the last thing anybody wanted was going into the hospital for elbow surgery and coming out of it with a positive case of COVID-19. Once the policies were lifted and surgeries were resumed, there was a massive backlog, putting an even heavier burden on hospital staffs as they caught up with the surge of demand.

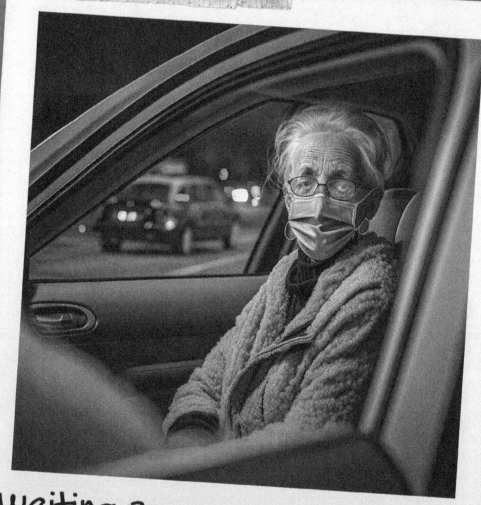

Waiting Rooms Were Replaced
With Patients Waiting
in Their Cars

The pandemic forced a drastic change in the traditional model of care delivery, especially regarding waiting rooms. To minimize patient contact and reduce the risk of viral transmission, dentists, clinics, and hospitals needed to avoid filling waiting rooms with patients.

The waiting room was typically the holding area for patients until they are ready to be seen. To keep their patients and their staff safe, these places started requesting that people stay in their own waiting rooms—their cars.

By being physically close to the facility but with a physical barrier around us, cars acted as virtual waiting rooms. An automated text message was sent the day before the appointment, instructing the patient to text back "READY" once they arrived and were parked. Sometimes a staff member would come out to check them in with a temperature reading and screening questions right at their car.

Other times, the patient was instructed to just remain in their car upon arrival. The system updated the patient status and sent text updates to notify them to when the doctor was ready to see them. It helped to keep the time lingering around the facility down to a minimum.

This simple and fully automated virtual waiting room solution was brilliant. They used familiar communication technology without the need for a patient portal or app. It also required minimal integration and could be launched quickly, making hospitals and clinics safer during the pandemic. It reduced the risk of viral transmission and freed up the staff from having to constantly maintain sanitization efforts within the building.

The only drawback was that patients could no longer pick up an old crusty Sports Illustrated magazine and read all about who won the 2003 Stanley Cup or pretend to read a magazine while peeping around at the other patients wondering, "I wonder what he's got…it can't be good."

41% of patients reported delaying care during the pandemic, due in part to a perceived additional risk factor on virus transmission. The waiting room on wheels helped to keep everyone safer.

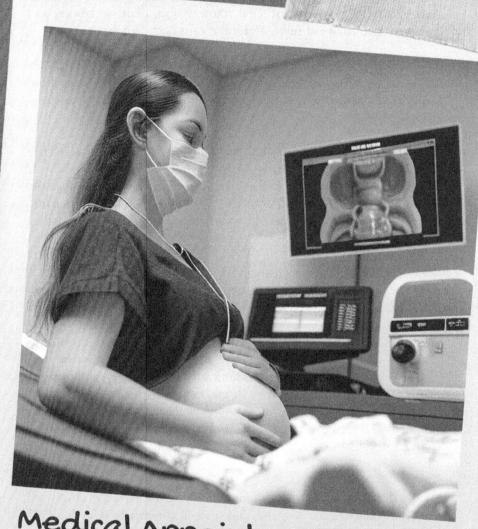

Medical Appointments Were Restricted to Just the Patient

One of the measures that was implemented in many clinics and hospitals was the restriction of visitors in certain areas, such as ultrasound departments, labor and delivery units, and surgical suites. This was done to limit the number of people in the facility at any given time, and to reduce exposure for patients, staff, and visitors.

Before the pandemic, clinics and hospitals had always had specific guidelines for visitors during appointments, surgeries, and child birthing. However, with the outbreak of COVID-19 in 2020, many clinics and hospitals enforced much tighter restrictions.

When women are going through a pregnancy, they require multiple, in-person clinic visits for measurements, exams, and lab tests to ensure the health of the mother and baby. For ultrasound and other prenatal measurement appointments, which were usually times of excitement, women commonly bring their partners, family, and children with to share in the moment. Many clinics and hospitals restricted additional people in the room or limited it to one.

In some cases, during child birth, only the expectant mother was allowed in the delivery room, while others allowed only one support person. Furthermore, individuals were required to wear masks during delivery. As a result, family members, doulas, and birth photographers (yes, this is thing) were left without access. After the delivery, visitors were restricted as well, leaving some mothers without the postpartum support they needed.

Although some hospitals had relaxed their policies, others continued to enforce restrictions that would change at any time depending on the pandemic's status. It was hard for expecting families to adequately construct a birthing plan, which in and of itself caused extra stress.

For other types of surgeries, the visitation limit was similar, allowing one or even no visitors for patients. For children having a surgery, that would mean picking which parent could stay with the child. For adult children, helping to get an elderly parent guided through a procedure proved to be difficult. While the restrictions were put in place to keep everyone safe, they caused extra stress for families.

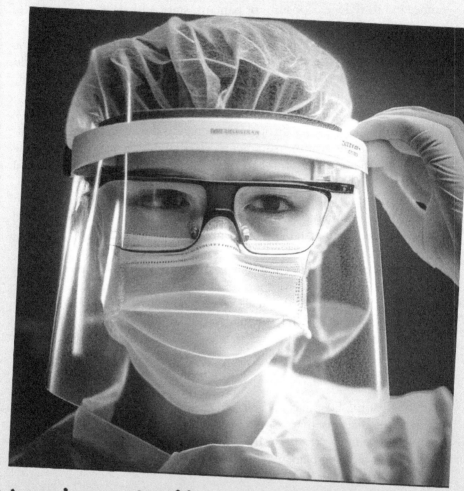

Nursing Staffs Were Pushed to the Limit

Out of everyone on the planet, frontline nurses were affected more than anybody during the pandemic. These healthcare professionals were at the forefront of the crisis, working tirelessly to care for patients and combat the spread of the virus. In the face of these challenges, nurses demonstrated remarkable courage and resilience.

One of the main challenges for front line nurses was high levels of stress and burnout. High-pressure working environments, long hours, high patient loads, and the constant threat of infection led to a significant increase in stress levels, with many nurses reporting feelings of anxiety, depression, and exhaustion.

Additionally, nurses working with COVID-19 patients were exposed to the physical risk of exposure to the virus and the mental difficulty of watching their patients battle with the disease. It was traumatizing.

Another challenge was the lack of personal protective equipment (PPE). In the early days of the pandemic, there were widespread shortages of PPE, particularly masks and gowns. This put nurses at an increased risk of infection, and many were forced to reuse or make do with inadequate equipment. During the early period of COVID-19, healthcare workers were hospitalized and died at rates that were atypically high for their ages and genders.

Nurses reported feeling isolated and disconnected from their colleagues, as well as from their families and loved one.

With limited visitation access for family members of Covid patients, it often fell to the nurses to use video calling to keep family members up to date on the status of their loved one. The long-term effects of the pandemic will be felt by front line nurses. Many nurses have reported that the experience affected their mental and physical health, and there is concern that the trauma of working during the pandemic may have long-lasting effects.

Despite these challenges, nurses showed amazingly remarkable courage and resilience in the face of the crisis, and their efforts saved countless lives and helped many others get back on their feet faster.

People Thought They Could Treat Covid-19 with Bleach

On April 23, 2020, President Trump took to the podium of the White House Briefing room. He had just heard Bill Bryan, head of science and technology at the Department of Homeland Security speak about virus half-lives, moving activities to outdoors, and the effectiveness of bleach, sunlight, and alcohol as disinfectants to kill the virus.

When President Trump came back to the podium, he added:

> "A question that probably some of you are thinking of if you're totally into that world, which I find to be totally interesting. So, supposing we hit the body with a tremendous —whether it's ultraviolet or just very powerful light—and I think you said that that hasn't been checked, but you're going to test it. And then I said, supposing you brought the light inside the body, which you can do either through the skin or in some other way, and I think you said you're going to test that, too. It sounds interesting. And then I see the disinfectant, where it knocks it out in a minute. One minute. And is there a way we can do something like that, by injection inside or almost a cleaning. Because you see it gets in the lungs, and it does a tremendous number on the lungs. So, it would be interesting to check that."

With that dumbfounding (and completely serious) statement, we witnessed the single highest level of misinformation of the pandemic. The very next day, amid a flurry of backlash and ridicule, President Trump retracted his proposal for scientists to test the injection of disinfectants and claimed he was being sarcastic. He wasn't.

After the briefing, several doctors spoke out against the President Trump's comments, deeming them irresponsible and extremely dangerous and they urgently cautioned the public about the severe consequences of consuming corrosive substances. The FDA put out a warning against using bleach as a treatment for COVID-19.

The American Association of Poison Control Centers said their bleach poisoning calls were up 38% and disinfectant poisoning calls were up 200% from the previous year. As it turns out, people don't need much convincing, and are quite capable of astonishing levels of stupidity.

Federal Government Contracted GE and Ford to Produce Ventilators

It's truly an admirable feat to see how our government officials can take decisive action during a crisis. And during the COVID-19 pandemic, there was no country better at taking decisive action than the United States. However, we might have overreacted just a tad bit.

In the face of the COVID-19 pandemic, we decided to order an astonishing 94,352 ventilators, just in case we needed them. On April 16, 2020, General Electric and Ford Motor partnered to produce 50,000 units and promised to have them delivered within 100 days.

In the initial stages of the COVID-19 crisis in March, health officials were alarmed about the expected scarcity of ventilators, which were critical in aiding patients' breathing and keeping them alive.

During April, medical professionals expressed concern that the government's ventilator orders would not be sufficient nor timely enough to address the anticipated surge in cases during the spring's initial peak. However, the infection curve persisted longer than anticipated, and medical practices have progressed.

The approach to treating COVID-19 changed during the months it took for companies to establish their supply chains, test prototypes, and train employees to manufacture the equipment. Medical experts learned more about the virus and how to treat it. This led to new treatments and protocols that helped to reduce the number of patients who needed to be put on ventilators. For example, the use of high-flow oxygen therapy and proning (placing patients on their stomachs) had been found to be effective in improving oxygenation in patients with COVID-19.

As it turns out, our hospitals never needed anywhere close to the number of emergency ventilators our government ordered. Most of the ventilators ended up sitting unused in warehouses collecting dust, while the cost of creating and maintaining them came in at well over $3 billion of taxpayer's money.

We can't blame ourselves for being too prepared. Better safe than sorry, right? It just meant wasting billions of dollars on equipment that will never be used. Wasting money is what the government is the very best at and they weren't going to let this golden opportunity pass them by.

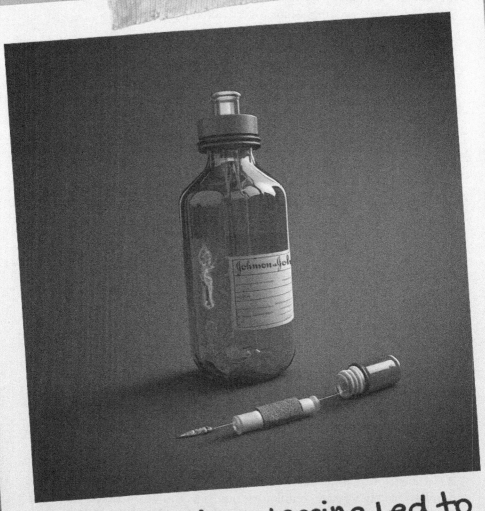

Fast Tracking Vaccine Led to Johnson & Johnson Version Being Paused

The COVID-19 pandemic led to a global race to develop and distribute vaccines as quickly as possible. One of the vaccines that was fast-tracked was the Johnson & Johnson vaccine, which was authorized for emergency use by the U.S Food and Drug Administration (FDA) in February 2021. However, the vaccine faced controversy and questions about its effectiveness, which led to a temporary halt in its use.

The Johnson & Johnson vaccine was a single-dose vaccine and considered a promising option for the U.S. vaccination campaign as it didn't require ultra-cold storage, which made it easier to distribute to rural and remote areas. However, after a small number of recipients developed a rare and severe blood clotting disorder, the Centers for Disease Control and Prevention (CDC) and the FDA recommended a temporary pause on the use of the vaccine.

The clotting disorder, called Cerebral Venous Sinus Thrombosis (CVST), occurred in combination with low platelets, which affected mostly women under 60, and was found to be more common in younger women.

After a thorough investigation, both the CDC and FDA cleared the Johnson & Johnson vaccine for emergency use again on April 23, 2021 with a warning that the vaccine could cause a rare but serious blood clot disorder, but also determined that the vaccine's benefits outweighed the risk of serious clotting disorders.

The situation with Johnson & Johnson vaccine highlighted the complexities of fast-tracking a vaccine during a pandemic. While it was important to move quickly to combat the spread of the virus, it was also essential to ensure the safety and efficacy of the vaccines. The pause in the use of the Johnson & Johnson was a cautionary tale. It also gave a lot of fuel to the anti-vaccine crowd, who thought that the vaccines were too unproven to widely adopt.

Entire books will be written around the way that we developed and rolled out the vaccines, the way anybody who questioned why people should take them if they are still going to be susceptible to the virus was struck down and silenced, and the way some employers forced employees to get vaccinated against their better judgements as a condition of employment. The Johnson & Johnson vaccine missteps will be just a single chapter in those book.

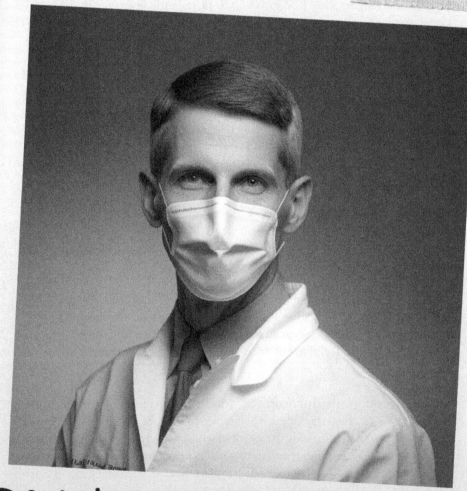

Dr. Anthony Fauci Flip-flopped on the Efficacy of Masks

The COVID-19 pandemic brought about a great deal of uncertainty and misinformation, which included the effectiveness of face masks. This led to a lot of confusion among the public about the appropriate use of masks, and people looked for guidance from health experts like Dr. Anthony Fauci, the director of the National Institute of Allergy and Infectious Diseases. However, Dr. Fauci's guidance on masks was a source of controversy, as he was perceived to have changed his position on the efficacy of masks multiple times during the pandemic.

During an interview on 60 Minutes in March 2020, Fauci stated that masks should be reserved for sick individuals as a means of source control, and he saw no need for healthy people to wear them while out and about. He said:

> "When you're in the middle of an outbreak, wearing a mask might make people feel a little bit better and it might even block a droplet, but it's not providing the perfect protection that people think that it is. And, often, there are unintended consequences—people keep fiddling with the mask and they keep touching their face."

As the scientific understanding of the virus improved and the data on the mode of transmission of COVID-19 was more understood, Dr. Fauci began to acknowledge the potential benefits of masks. In April 2020, Dr. Fauci stated that masks could be helpful in slowing the spread of the virus, but that they were not a substitute for other public health measures such as social distancing. He also stated that the decision to wear a mask should be based on local conditions and the level of virus transmission in each community.

In July 2020, Dr. Fauci changed his position again, stating that masks should be worn universally, regardless of the level of transmission in each community. He now claimed masks were an effective tool in slowing the spread and preventing a resurgence of COVID-19 cases.

The flip-flopping on masks was a source of confusion and frustration among the public, as well as a topic of political and social debate, and his seemingly political ulterior motives sowed seeds of distrust in him.

About the Author

Anthony Faust is a web developer and graphic designer, who loves all things pop culture. He is married, is a father of two, and lives in the Minneapolis/St. Paul suburbs which makes him a big fan of all of the Minnesota sports teams. His favorite TV series of all-time is The Wire and his favorite movie of all-time is Back to the Future II. He has no political affiliations or aspirations.

This is his debut book.

Made in the USA
Las Vegas, NV
05 May 2024

89561322R00134